Praise for WIN AGAIN!

"WIN AGAIN is a great resource not only for me, but for the hundreds of athletes who I'm providing much of Mark's career advice to through my VIKTRE and NexGoal websites. Mark truly understands what is required to get an athlete up off the couch and into the office, and delivers his tips in an easy step-by-step way that we can all absorb and use immediately. I not only recommend that my athlete clients read WIN AGAIN, but urge you to read it too, it will definitely jumpstart your career!"

~ Kevin Dahl, NHL and Olympian

"WIN AGAIN is well organized and easy to read. Some of the advice covers things that I've already been doing, which is good, but there is a lot of great info in the book that really caught my attention because it is so simple to do, and clearly is advice that nobody else seems to be using or teaching. I like the fact that Mark gets right to the point, and doesn't go on too long when trying to get his strategies across. If you want to have the edge when competing for your next great position, this is the resource to go to, and Mark is just the guy to deliver it."

~ Michael Moriarty, MLB Player, Coach and Scout

"I wish I had WIN AGAIN to use as a guide while I was playing and even after I retired. Mark makes it very easy for all current and retired athletes to follow his guidance to transition into business. In fact, I've been using his strategies now to boost my current speaking business. You will see that Mark's tips will benefit you not just now but for years to come. Make sure this is the next book you read!"

~ Theoren Fleury, NHL All-Star and Olympian

"I retired in 2004 as an Olympian in rowing after many years of training, and the transition into the working world was quite challenging. I wish I had this book back then, as WIN AGAIN is the ultimate playbook for athletes who aspire to be as successful in business as they were in sport. Mark's insightful methodology demystifies the process and makes it easy for any athlete to approach what is typically the very difficult transition from sport to career. Mark provides an easy to follow roadmap for helping athletes translate the characteristics that made them successful on the field to those that will make them successful in business. WIN AGAIN is a must read for all athletes at every stage of their careers."

~ Garrett Klugh, Olympic Rower

"I think the book is terrific. Its playbook format makes it easy to learn, follow, and understand the content. Even the title - "WIN AGAIN" translates to the individual in transition who has achieved success before and is now entering uncharted territory. I used some insight from Chapter 3 just yesterday with a former NBA Player sharing with him the aspect of "Play to your strengths". I am all over Chapter 7 - I just assisted former NBA Player Keyon Dooling with his LinkedIn page on Monday and he jumped from 1st to 5th gear immediately! Chapter 9 is the area that all professional athletes need to master. For the platform they are on and the exposure they get - if you can network correctly - there are no doors that you can't open. One more thing - "Write an article - it's much easier than you think" - Professional athletes have so many mediums they can use to share their story - JUST DO (WRITE) IT!!! Mark, thanks for writing a resource that I can use repeatedly with the players and coaches that I support both within and outside the NBA."

~ Stephen Eriksen, Director of Players Programs / Engagement, Adonal Foyle Enterprises

"I finished WIN AGAIN and loved it! The resources that Mark shared about finding opportunities, following up, LinkedIn and negotiating offers really resonated with me. It wasn't easy finding my way after retiring from the Olympics, and having this as a job search tool will only help going forward for the rest of my career. Thanks, Mark!"

~ Keeth Smart, Olympic Silver Medalist, Fencing and Co-Founder / COO, Physiclo

"As a professional athlete, it isn't an easy transition moving from something that you love and have done your whole life to starting all over and finding a new career in your mid 30's. It is a challenge in so many ways. This is why I strongly recommend that every athlete, whether active or retired, take advantage of Mark's immense knowledge and experience, read WIN AGAIN, and go through his Career Coaching Program. His coaching is personalized, thorough, and gives you a plan on how to network in a smart and professional way. His attention to detail and proven strategies have been so helpful, with his best piece of advice being how to use LinkedIn to your great advantage. His guidance and simple plan opened up a whole new world on how to find the people and opportunities that I was looking for. I truly believe that it doesn't matter if you are a former athlete, experienced executive, or a recent college graduate, if you are looking for a new career it is definitely important and necessary to have a coach to guide and help you through an uneasy process that can be quite intimidating and humbling at times. WIN AGAIN gives you a strategy and purpose to what you are doing, and not just constantly doing the same things over and over that don't yield any results. I would highly recommend Mark to anyone looking for impactful and truly effective career advice and coaching."

~ Greg Johnson, NHL and Olympian

WIN AGAIN!

WIN AGAIN!

TURN ATHLETIC EXCELLENCE INTO BUSINESS SUCCESS

The Job Search Playbook

Mark Moyer

ISBN - 9780999387108
ISBN: 0999387103
Library of Congress Control Number: 2017914591
Mark Moyer, New York, NY

This book is dedicated to my wife and best friend Lisa, who's witnessed the ups and downs of my entrepreneurial spirit, and offered her tremendous expertise about the corporate landscape--a vast library of knowledge available anytime under our own roof.

My kids, Jack, Veronica and Ryan, who are amazed and excited that their dad wrote this book. I'm fully confident that they'll take much of this advice to heart as they seek out the jobs and careers of their dreams.

And to Duke, who through all of this has remained faithfully by my side, always ready with a tail wag when I hit the occasional roadblock.

Table of Contents

INTRODUCTION

*"I've played baseball my whole life, and I know I can do
that well. I can compete with anyone at anything physically.
But when your body goes, what do you do then?
You have to totally reinvent yourself."*

~ MIKE HAMPTON, MLB ALL-STAR

IMAGINE A STADIUM FILLED WITH retired amateur and professional athletes. How many of them, do you think, have transitioned to a satisfying business career? My educated guess: barely enough to field one team. That's too many on the sidelines and not enough in the game!

Most retired athletes struggle to reinvent themselves after years of complete immersion in what they believe they were born to do. And all those high school and college athletes who are banking on going pro... what happens to the ones who aren't chosen?[1]

If you're reading this book, you most likely feel unsure about what direction to take now that you've graduated or retired from the game you love. You may be wondering who will want to hire you or what you're

---

[1] A recent NCAA report shows that the odds of making it onto a professional major sports roster are nearly impossible. Of 1.1 million high school football players, just 6.8 % made it onto any division level NCAA football team, and of that 6.8%, only 1.5% of those draft-eligible were drafted. http://www.ncaa.org/sites/default/files/2015-16RES_ Probability_Chart_Web_20170314.pdf

qualified to do outside your sport…telling yourself you're unprepared for the challenges of the job market, let alone the demands of the job.

Those of you who played professionally were revered by your fans, rewarded financially more than you could have imagined, and able to take advantage of your natural talents. You're used to people "yes-ing" you at every turn and agents taking care of your needs. Now, overnight, that's all gone. The team you played for last may have held a retirement ceremony or party on your behalf, but suddenly they're off the grid, while your agent is looking for the next talent to represent. Your family life is different too, as you're always home instead of being away for chunks of time. Everyone needs to adjust.

If you were an amateur, collegiate or Olympic athlete, you spent most of your free time training for the sport you love. You used your formative years to improve and dominate in your sport. There was little time left to dedicate to education, much less to personal relationships that could benefit you in a professional life outside of the game.

The transition from athlete to employee can seem rough.

But it doesn't have to be that way.

TURN YOUR ATHLETIC ADVANTAGE INTO BUSINESS SUCCESS

Whether you've played professional sports, spent time on a college or high school team, or just see yourself as a weekend warrior, your athletic background has made you an exceptional candidate for any number of exciting jobs, and your training, mindset and past performance can be the building blocks and differentiators for your next brilliant career.

Now that you've left the field, court, rink or arena behind, and you're facing the daunting prospect of finding your place in an unfamiliar world, you're in the same position as tens of thousands of unhappy employees, career changers and recent grads.

But you've got years of experience tackling opponents, outrunning competition and crossing finish lines.

And that's not all--you've got this book. Which means you have the best kind of home-court advantage: someone pulling for you who has the knowledge and experience to help you transition successfully out of sports and into the business world.

What I'm about to show you is a practical, step-by-step method for finding and landing your ideal job by combining skills you already have with techniques I've developed over 25 years of executive recruiting and coaching. I'll teach you how to develop a powerful network you can leverage throughout your entire working life. I'll describe the best way to present yourself: how to create and promote your "brand."

You'll learn powerful techniques for turning strangers into allies; strategies for connecting with influencers; and a proven process for getting contacts to recommend you to the hiring manager who can offer you the position you want most. You'll become a world-class networker and a first-string interviewer--the kind of candidate decision-makers recognize as exactly what they need.

Is this book for you?

The WIN AGAIN method was designed for anyone transitioning from one work environment to another. Its key message is that you can reinvent yourself and find success *without giving up what has made you feel inspired, challenged and gratified up until now.*

This book is for:

* **Current or retired professional athletes:** If it's time for a big change but you don't know where to begin, *WIN AGAIN* will show you how to launch your first season in the business world, while continuing to leverage your brand as an athlete.

- **College players who won't be going pro:** If you haven't figured out where to go next or how to get there, this book will help you target your ideal industry, company and position, and get you in the best shape to beat your competition for the job.
- **Amateur athletes with a demonstrated commitment to a sport:** If you played on a high school team or even on your own time, *WIN AGAIN* will teach you how to turn your history of hard work, clear focus and competitive spirit into a proven formula for business success.
- **Job seekers, career changers and anyone struggling to find their ideal place in the working world:** Even if you're not inclined to swing a bat or kick a ball, but you're unhappy in your job or you want to change careers, you can use the plan laid out in these pages to define your brand and present yourself to hiring managers as the solution to the problems they most need to solve.

You might not know what kind of job you want. You might think you're not qualified for the positions that interest you. Maybe you're convinced you have no contacts in the business community. On all these issues and more, I've got your back.

In summary, this book is for you if:

- You're waking up to the realization that it's time for a major change. You need to let go of your "glory days" and make your mark in the business world.
- You miss the thrill of playing on a school team—you're afraid you'll never feel that excitement again.
- You've opened a new chapter in your professional life. It's going okay, but you know there's something better out there—you're just not sure how to go after it.

* You're having a hard time taking charge of your career without the structure, discipline and guidance of a "coach" and a plan you can trust.

There's a well-kept secret for standing out in today's employment market and I'm going to reveal it to you here. Most job-hunters today are still using old, obsolete methods. They have no idea how the game has changed. They're still playing by the old rules.

To prevail in this new arena, you need a winning mindset, a compelling personal narrative, a professional network and a system for putting your story in front of the people who can get you hired.

This book will tell you how to develop all of those. It will also serve as your virtual "coach" to keep you strong and focused as you work through the process. *WIN AGAIN* will introduce you to an innovative approach, and hand you everything you need to make it work. I'm going to lay out the exact steps to take, with examples, tips and templates that will get you off the bench and keep you moving forward for as long as you choose to work.

WHAT YOU WON'T FIND HERE

You won't be asked to draw soul-searching diagrams or take detailed personality tests. No navel gazing here--just simple steps, straight-shooting advice and proven techniques to help you take actions that drive results. *WIN AGAIN* is not about sending out hundreds of resumes, applying to jobs that have likely already been filled, and sitting around waiting for a response that never comes. It's a proactive method for deciding what kind of job you want, then reaching out to the people who can help you get it, and making sure they see right away what you bring to the table. It puts you in charge of your own future, starting now. No waiting, no whining, no wasting time.

Let's hit the field!

If it seems like you're drifting on a raft in the middle of the ocean, this book will be your lifeline, as well as a compass and map to guide you as you navigate your career and discover why, where and with whom you should be working. Whether you live in a lavish home with plenty of toys parked in the driveway, or you're struggling to get the bills paid, I want you to close your eyes (*it's fine if you don't, I'm not watching*), and imagine what it would be like to wake up each morning with purpose, feeling relevant, and not only drawing a paycheck, but contributing in ways that keep you challenged, energized and excited to be back on a team.

Follow the plan laid out in this book, and that vision can become your new life.

FIRST QUARTER
TAKE STOCK

CHAPTER 1

TIME TO MOVE ON

*"They teach you how to play the game, but
they don't teach you how to leave it."*

~ GORDIE HOWE, NHL HALL OF FAMER, "MR. HOCKEY"

YOUR GLORY DAYS--ARE THEY OVER?

YOU PROBABLY STARTED PLAYING SPORTS when you were very young. I bet when you were asked what you wanted to be, you either answered, "baseball player for the Yankees!" or "quarterback for the 49ers!" I doubt you said, "I want to be smart, funny, giving, successful, and--oh yeah, an athlete."

By middle and high school, you'd been committed to at least one sport, and may have shifted your focus to a specific one in which, with years of training, you achieved success. Sports were everything, and there was very little life outside of them. Your friends, family and those who knew you labeled you as a jock because of how you dressed and your sleeping, eating, fitness and socializing habits. This label follows you around even now, and you wonder how you can shed it to be viewed as a hirable candidate.

Those of us who expressed a passion (and sometimes a talent) for sports developed a highly competitive nature. I get it—to this day, I won't let my kids beat me at anything unless they earn that win. I'm an insufferable competitor and I'm sure you are too. We were patted on the back when we told everyone we'd be in the big leagues someday. The problem is that you learned to see yourself only as an athlete aiming for the pros, not as an individual with untapped potential and a wide range of abilities, who also happens to kick butt in a sport.

If you were lucky enough to go pro or play in college, everyone assumes you've got lots going for you: tremendous drive, leadership skills, a strong work ethic, a public persona, maybe even an army of fans. Seems like you're on top of the world. So why do you feel like your best days are behind you?

You miss the camaraderie, the daily training routine, practices, games, meetings, meals--everything planned down to the minute. And now your livelihood, your future and your family may depend on you figuring out where to go from here.

You've still got a big game to play

As an athlete, you've set goals, overcome obstacles, celebrated victories and weathered defeats. You've empowered, motivated or led others to bring out their best. You've kept to tight schedules, shown up and fought hard to improve, trained your mind and your reflexes to stay focused and strong. How many job candidates can say the same? And what company doesn't want someone like that on its payroll?

Each of you has been a committed "employee" since you were a child, putting enormous time and effort into becoming an extraordinary athlete, and that alone demonstrates a superior level of engagement most hiring managers will value. You've also proven yourself to be a coachable team player with specialized skills: a determined competitor who never takes his or her eyes off the prize.

Are you comfortable in front of the camera, addressing the media or speaking to large crowds? There are roles in broadcasting, public relations, sales and business development that non-athletes who struggle in front of an audience might be less qualified to fill.

Do you have the discipline to follow a pre-determined strategy? The presence of mind to make split-second decisions? You could be just what they need on the trading floor.

Did you motivate your teammates to a victory that seemed out of reach? Leadership and management capabilities are essential in the boardroom.

These are just some of the qualities many "civilian" job seekers don't possess.

OK, that's the good news: there's a lot you can contribute right off the bat. Now I need to get you up to the plate. But first, a quick anecdote to put things in perspective.

The Win Again Playbook: why it blows away the competition

After graduating college, I spent a year in California waiting tables, working at a sporting goods store, and hearing my surfer friends ask, "Dude... why are you walking so fast?"

I'd been raised in Connecticut, schooled in upstate New York, and always had the need to get from point A to point B in record time. Must have been the athlete in me. I shifted from California's Manhattan Beach to Manhattan, NY and started searching for a job in finance. It wasn't a good time for that sort of thing--I'm talking 1987, just after the crash.

One day, my former roommate got a call about a sales job. He'd moved out--I had no idea to where--and the person on the phone was looking for salespeople. I stepped up and interviewed for the job myself. Selling office copiers door-to-door. For the next thirteen months, I got doors slammed in my face from nine to five. Pretty miserable way to spend the day.

Fortunately, in that time, I learned a lot more than how to sell. I learned how to translate my skills and interests into a career I've loved for the past 25 years. The insights I gained showed me how to repair the disconnect between what I had to offer and the jobs I was settling for. Those thirteen months were training camp and when it was over I knew how to interact with people, eliminate objections, and turn rejection into opportunity.

The idea that it was up to me, that I could chart a professional course that would keep me happy and fulfilled, not only led me to become a recruiter, it formed the bedrock of my approach and completely raised my game.

Here's one of the most valuable pieces of advice I can offer: Be proactive.

You've got to take charge of the process yourself or you'll spend your life reacting. Taking what lands on you. Knocking on doors that never open.

Choosing to become a recruiter was just the beginning for me. I wanted to learn all aspects of job-hunting and uncover the best-kept secrets to building a successful, satisfying, long-lasting career.

I realized I was only focusing on half the picture. As a recruiter, I put myself in the shoes of hiring managers so they would make my candidate an offer. A hiring manager wants to know: "Can your candidate solve my problems?" The recruiter's job is to help him answer "yes." It's not about what's best for the candidate in the long run. It's about landing him or her *that* job. How does the position fit into the bigger picture of the candidate's life and career? Not the recruiter's concern.

To understand and master both sides of the process, I needed to come at it from the candidate's perspective too. That's why I became a career coach as well as a recruiter. I learned how to strategize for candidates, to help them identify their ideal position and then take all the right steps to go after it.

I created a system for both landing a job immediately and for growing a career over decades. I designed a clear, actionable blueprint for networking and interviewing, and showed candidates how to keep their energy high, their intentions directed and their motivation strong.

In other words, I developed the game plan you're reading now.

My first professional athlete client was Greg Johnson, a 13-year NHL player, team captain and Olympic medalist. After doing something he loved and had done all his life, he was finding it difficult to start over and forge a new career in his mid-thirties. He was intimidated by how he'd be perceived in the business world, and concerned about how his LinkedIn profile compared to candidates already making a name for themselves. He said, "Mark, there's no way I can beat these people out for an interview, much less an offer. I don't have many of the skills that would interest a hiring manager."

We went through my coaching program and he soon landed a job on an equity trading desk, where he remains thrilled to be to this day. In Greg's words, my guidance and simple plan "opened up a whole new world on how to find the people and opportunities I was looking for."

My experience with Greg introduced me to a population that was largely ignored, but perfectly positioned to take advantage of what I had to teach.

As a lifelong sports-lover and athlete myself, I had analyzed the qualities I could bring to a job, traits that drew me to sports in the first place, as well as those I'd developed on the court, on the field and in the rink. Now I could apply my career-building techniques to the specific circumstances of transitioning athletes.

Soon, more pro-athletes became my clients, and before long I knew I had a highly-effective formula for turning a sports-minded background into a confident attitude, a winning skill set and a fulfilling post-athletic career.

Most job hunters today waste hours, days, even years poring over job boards and sending resumes into the void. I can't stress enough: that doesn't work! Companies don't hire the way they used to. There's a hidden job market now with its own unwritten rules. I spent years figuring out this new game and then helped hundreds of people win at it: by following my step-by-step method, they found the right job in the right company, the job that draws on their unique talents and brings out the best in them. The one that has them eager to get out of bed and go to work.

The dual perspective of recruiter and coach is hard to find--many people think I'm crazy to practice both at the same time. But that's exactly why my *WIN AGAIN* playbook has been so effective. It functions at the intersection of what hiring managers need and what candidates want. And that's where career magic happens.

THE GAME PLAN

The *WIN AGAIN* playbook takes you through four phases.

In Part 1, *Take Stock*, you'll assess your skills and align them with your interests. You'll learn how to recognize your ideal job, and develop a mind-set that will keep you winning throughout your career.

In Part 2, *Identify your Targets*, you'll define your brand and tell your story. Then I'll help you decide what industries, companies and positions suit you best, and create a list of specific positions to target. I'll show you an easy way to identify jobs that intrigue you and work environments in which you're most likely to thrive. And I'll reveal my secrets for unlocking a wealth of job-hunting information that most people have no idea exists.

In Part 3, *Grow Your Network*, you'll find an easy-to-follow plan for reaching out to experts, influencers and hiring managers. You'll master techniques that turn acquaintances (even strangers) into fans who will re-fer and endorse you. You'll become a pro at following up by phone and in person, and knowing how to uncover exactly what hiring managers are looking for. I'll explain why you should never offer someone your resume and I'll tell you how to make people think recommending you was their idea. In today's market, it's all about who you know!

In Part 4, *Ace Your Interviews and Land Your Offers*, you'll learn how to show your interviewers you've got exactly what they need. You'll discover tricks for getting your contacts to reveal the best questions to ask and the right answers to prepare. *WIN AGAIN* will set you up to walk in with confidence, perform at the top of your game and bring it home. And once you land that dream job, you'll have my best tips on how to negotiate a contract and continue growing your network as you cultivate your career.

Along the way, you'll see occasional sidebars or text boxes with additional information. Here's what they mean:

Power play: A strategy or move that puts you ahead of the competition.

Coach says: Tips to motivate you and keep you on track.

Foul!: Stuff to watch out for and things you shouldn't do.

You got this!: Something your athletic training has prepared you to do well.

Here's how: A quick recap of steps in a recommended process.

Although you may feel like you've passed your prime, your years of dedication to one or several sports have taught you skills you've never acknowledged, brought you strengths you haven't measured and prepared you far better than you realize for successes that lie ahead.

CHAPTER 2

MANAGE YOUR MINDSET

"The first training camp that I missed, I was like, 'Jeez, what am I going to do now?' Jackie Robinson said that athletes die twice. You know, when that first career is gone, that's a death."

~ KAREEM ABDUL–JABBAR, NBA HALL OF FAMER

IT AMAZES ME HOW MANY people I speak with have a negative attitude about their job search, their prospects, and their ability to create and maintain professional relationships that can move their careers forward. Over and over, I've seen their mindset change dramatically once they start implementing strategies to outpace the competition, and realize they have a very good chance of being hired for their ideal job.

The process becomes much easier when you go into it with the belief that you deserve the job of your dreams. You stand out, even among those who seem more qualified, because your positive approach wins over hiring managers who are drawn to your enthusiasm and immediately see the upside of adding you to their team.

GETTING YOUR GAME FACE ON

You know how important it is to get ready before the whistle blows. That's why the first step in the *WIN AGAIN* process is mental preparation. As you consider the prospect of making a change, take a moment to examine your mindset.

Are you telling yourself any of these negative stories?

* I'm not qualified for any role in the business world
* I'm too old to change careers
* The job market is terrible right now
* I'll never beat the competition
* I have no idea what I want to do
* I don't have the right connections
* I don't even know where to begin

Let's rephrase these ideas as specific job-searching challenges that have practical solutions. Then we can talk about how you'll get around them.

AM I QUALIFIED?

I bet many of you are following this common (misguided) approach: you read job descriptions and compare your skills or experience to the stated requirements for the position. You scan through (or pore over) a list of tasks and decide you'll never be hired because you haven't done *exactly* those things. The ad says they're looking for three to five years' experience and you don't have it. The description references titles that have never been yours. The job you're dreaming of seems out of your league and you're thinking you might as well forget it.

Time Out!

Many job descriptions are written deliberately to turn candidates away.

A company may be legally required to publicize an opening, but already have someone in mind for the job.

Internal recruiters and hiring managers often have to slog through mountains of resumes, so they write postings designed to discourage applicants and whittle down their stack of candidates for review.

You haven't even begun to explore the possibilities that can grow out of your abilities and interests. In addition, it's not just about what you've done in the past, it's also about what you want to do in the future. The answer is not to match yourself to existing descriptions but to describe yourself in ways that will open doors.

In the coming chapters, you'll see that you qualify for far more positions than you could have imagined. And you'll learn how to make that clear to the person considering your application.

It's not only about what you've done--it's about what you can and want to do.

AM I TOO OLD?

Some of the people I coach are nearing retirement age (although I'm not sure what number that is these days!). Many fear age discrimination and hesitate to put dates on their resume or LinkedIn profile, assuming people will do the math. They don't post a picture on LinkedIn because they're afraid they look old.

If that's what you're thinking--let it go!

Some of us are old and getting older, and there's very little we can do to hide that fact. There's a silver lining (other than the one in your hair) that should be obvious, although you may not be thinking about it today.

YOU HAVE MUCH-NEEDED WISDOM AND EXPERTISE

Maybe you've seen lots of markets go up and down. Dealt with highly-charged circumstances or difficult co-workers. You may be more comfortable handling stressful situations than millennials or those just coming out of school.

If you're using outdated advice that worked well in the "good old days" but clearly isn't coming through for you now, your job search probably feels like a burdensome exercise with no clear light at the end of the tunnel. As your frustration mounts, it's tempting to come up with excuses for why you're not getting any meetings, interviews or offers. And the most convenient excuse of all could be your age.

Candidates have a habit of diminishing, discrediting or simply ignoring much of what they can offer to prospective hiring managers. That needs to change! You'll soon be learning interview strategies that will showcase your expertise and reduce concerns anybody may have about your age. If you're older, embrace it and make it work to your advantage!

I'LL NEVER GET HIRED IN THIS MARKET!

I'm often asked, "Hey Mark, how's the job market? Are companies hiring? Is there a lot of competition? Why does it seem so tough to find a job?"

I have a simple, direct answer to those questions: **Who cares how the job market is these days!**

If it's cranking along with tons of opportunities, if companies are staffing up like crazy, that just means you have tons of competition. If the market is slow or dead and virtually nobody's hiring, your competition will be substantially lighter and companies will not see as many qualified candidates. How many jobs do you need? Just one, right? Don't worry about how good or bad the market is. I don't care and you shouldn't either. Let's focus on getting you that dream job you deserve.

LEAVE YOUR COMPETITION IN THE DUST

In addition to worrying that they lack qualifications, many of my clients are concerned that a multitude of other candidates will match or exceed the requirements for a position.

Take a step back and think: do you know friends, family, former colleagues or anyone else who's been hired while seeming to lack virtually every "necessary" skill or ability needed for that job? Of course you do--so do I!

Every day, thousands of people are chosen because they demonstrate that they'll be a strong fit for the role not just today but for the long haul. These people beat out their competition not because they have more experience, not because they're smarter, not because they're better looking, and not for other reasons you may think are holding you back.

How do they pull it off?

They win over those hiring managers with other intangibles: for example, their ability to run a project in adverse circumstances; their specific knowledge of an area the company wants to grow into; or the way they bond personally and professionally with the decision-makers.

As for the last three objections (not knowing what you want or how to go after it, and believing you don't have the right connections), we'll address all of those very soon.

No matter what happens, don't do this!

For retired professional athletes, there's an elephant in the room: make sure your celebrity doesn't give you a bad attitude! As a job seeker, you need to inspire as much good will as possible—nobody wants an arrogant or condescending co-worker. Potential managers or colleagues may be thrilled just to meet you, but they might also feel intimidated by your fame. Treating them as equals will not only present you as a more likeable candidate but set you up for strong relationships once you've been hired.

Think like a winner

If your goal is to land a position in a career you had not previously thought possible, you'll be far more likely to succeed if you go into the process with the right frame of mind.

Here are some things you can do, in addition to adjusting your attitude, that will help you stay focused and directed in your search.

ESTABLISH A DAILY ROUTINE

One of the aspects you may miss from your days as an athlete is your daily routine. While you were training and competing, you had a set time to wake up, eat your breakfast, exercise, study game day materials, eat lunch, work out again, attend meetings, go to dinner, maybe squeeze in another workout and then lights out, only to repeat it all again the next day. The sooner you establish a new routine, even while conducting a job search, the better frame of mind you'll maintain.

If you're currently out of work or working part time, you'll need a routine that incorporates a somewhat healthy diet (there are plenty of other books that can help you with that!), an exercise program that keeps you active, the right amount of sleep, and time to invest in your job search.

DEVELOP EFFECTIVE JOB-SEARCHING HABITS

If you're lucky, your job search will feel more like a sprint than a marathon, but either way it will demand consistent effort. To boost your productivity and stick with the program, I recommend setting clear, measurable goals for yourself on a daily and weekly basis. These might include a minimum number of hours spent or actions taken. Obviously, some days will be more productive than others, but draw on your years of productive routine to make your job search more effective.

IT'S UP TO YOU!

Whether you're concerned about your age, your qualifications or your competition, you can use these tips to stand out and feel confident.

1) Focus on your job search and not on your emotions. Lose any anger you have about being laid off or feeling ignored because of your age. There's no way to get around it, so use it to your advantage.

2) Look the part. It's amazing how much farther you'll get if you dress for success and give the impression that you have the knowledge and wisdom to perform the job well.

3) Stay current with technology and your industry. I'll be giving you tips on how to go about this, as well as on following new trends.

4) Bolster your network. You'll be astounded by what a strong network can do for you. We'll get down and dirty on how to set up and grow a robust network that will help you now and for the rest of your career.

5) Get comfortable answering the question: *"What do you do?"* and be ready to clearly articulate your skills and capabilities. We'll talk more about that soon.

6) Put yourself in the place of the people you speak to or meet. Anticipate any preconceived notions or prejudices they may have about your age and put those at ease as soon as possible.

7) Hire a career coach! Going through the job search process on your own can be incredibly challenging. A coach will partner with you to assess your capabilities, adjust your expectations, and tighten up skills that may have softened over the years, such as interviewing and following up. Coaches are uniquely qualified to develop a job-search strategy that will lead you towards your professional goals so you can advance your career instead of settling for a job to pay the bills.

The bottom line is that every job seeker has issues to address before becoming a winning candidate, and there's little reason why you can't be the person landing the job and accepting the offer.

In today's employment market, people chart their own course: there's no longer a direct line from an academic degree to a particular position. This is great news if you're moving between unrelated professions, like from hockey to public relations or football to finance. It means that *you* paint the picture and connect the dots. It's up to you to show them who you are and what you can do for them.

While I can't guarantee specific results, I can confidently tell you that if you meet or exceed the goals I lay out in this book, you'll catch up to and overtake the job seekers around you who are not following the *WIN AGAIN* playbook.

CHAPTER 3

REVIEW YOUR HIGHLIGHT REEL

"Know your strengths and take advantage of them."

~ GREG NORMAN, WORLD GOLF HALL OF FAMER, "THE SHARK"

I CRINGE EVERY TIME SOMEONE tells me, "Mark, the market is so bad right now, I'll take whatever it gives me. *I'd settle for anything.*"

Many job seekers feel this way. I understand where it comes from, so let me say this loudly: **Settling is a total waste of time**!

It may sound unrealistic or even absurd, but the smart, practical thing to do is pursue the job you want most. As I'll show you over the next few chapters, your best chance of getting hired and succeeding in your career is to target the position that suits you best. You'll be enthusiastic, you'll stay motivated, you'll want to trample any opposition and leap over every hurdle. Here's the bottom line:

Spend every moment of your search going after your "dream job."

Most job seekers go about this all wrong. They put their hope in the job boards...follow bad advice from well-meaning friends, relatives and colleagues...fire off resumes left and right like a series of Hail-Mary passes. Even worse, many people just wing it and let fate dictate their next move.

They don't realize that the ball is in their court. That they need to make hiring managers choose *them*--by identifying their strengths, aligning their skills with their interests and combining all of that into a package that sells.

So how do you figure out what you want to do?

SET THE BAR HIGH

Some folks muscle through decades of awful jobs before they find out what interests them and where they want to work. They stay stuck. They don't move. Similarly, it can feel like an uphill battle to decide what's next after enjoying the life of an athlete.

Don't give up! Avoid the passive approach, where you:

* sit at your computer for hours, reading semi-interesting job descriptions.
* ask your friends what jobs appeal to them and see if you feel the same way.
* stare at the wall of your home or local Starbucks and think up opportunities that *won't* just magically appear.

As an athlete, you know that setting the bar high pushes you to redefine yourself and your abilities. It inspires you to exceed expectations.

If you were a team member or a draft pick, you're used to playing to your strengths.

Think about it:

Do you pass on the curve ball and wait to crush the fastball? Go early to the net because you know that's where you shine? Maybe you're not the biggest guy on the field but you've got tremendous speed,

> **You got this!**
>
> Setting the bar high pushes you to redefine yourself and your abilities. It inspires you to exceed expectations.

allowing you to evade your defender on your way to scoring the touchdown.

You've not only figured out your strengths, you've put them to work. What we're going to do next is a variation on that theme.

Are you ready?

Play to your strengths

We all know of athletes, performers and public figures who've made a name for themselves with a signature talent or skill set. As a job seeker, you'll take a similar approach.

Our next step, which I call the **Personal Strengths Tracker,** coaches you through the process of identifying your strongest, most gratifying skills and using them as the foundation of your brand.[2] I'm about to hand you the building blocks for landing your next ideal job, so **do not skip this step!** Consider it your training to get to the big leagues.

When I work with athletes and professionals, the first thing I have them do is break things down to their simplest components. You want to ferret out the obvious details (even though they may not seem obvious yet): key information about you, your career and what ultimately makes you tick. Start by answering the question: **What have you done within your athletic career, your business or your personal life that has made you feel happy, challenged and successful?**

Do a deep dive. Most of us have never tried this, but you'll see right away how it sheds light on what you'll bring to a future employer. **What have you done that you're most proud of? When have you made a positive impact that left you feeling great about yourself?** Many of us have these experiences but never connect them to our current career or job search. But you should. *It's the simplest way to figure out what you're good at.*

---

[2] This tool is based on GetFive's Seven Stories Exercise, which was inspired by Bernard Haldane's work in the 1940s to help military veterans transition to the civilian workforce.

LIST YOUR TROPHY MOMENTS

Pull out some paper and start creating a list. When you were a teenager, did you lead a group of Boy Scouts up a mountain, drawing on your leadership skills to help them push past their comfort zones and make it to the top? While training for the sports you played, did you overcome challenges and even injuries so you could compete or finish a race? As a child, did you build a sandcastle that won a contest, showcasing talent in architecture and design? Over the course of your career, you may have nailed a project, reduced a budget or written a report that impressed others (and yourself). Consider your volunteer work and your hobbies…have you achieved anything there that stands out in your mind?

Remember that these should be meaningful to *you*, not necessarily to your friends, family, teammates or co-workers. It doesn't matter if hardly anyone knows about these accomplishments. You're looking for moments that made you proud. Times when you would have given yourself an award or a trophy!

If you're thinking: "I really have no idea what my accomplishments are," it's likely you're struggling because of one or more of the following:

1. Your accomplishments may be tough to measure because they're more qualitative than quantitative.
2. People around you don't show appreciation for what you've done.
3. You underestimate what you have to offer. You don't realize that with your knowledge and expertise, you can outshine the competition.

PLAYBOOK

I was at a networking event recently and noticed a man in his 50s, and his name tag said "Insurance Rep."

I commented that it must be challenging to approach strangers and ask for their money and trust. He concurred, admitting he was going through a rough stretch, and quite frankly, he looked pretty beat up. I asked if he was involved in decision-making about how to invest the money he brought in. He said he was. I followed by asking if he thought his selections would outperform the market and he told me they usually did.

I said, "Don't call yourself an insurance rep--you're a financial strategist!" He nearly dropped his drink and exclaimed, "That's the single best piece of advice I've ever gotten at a networking event!"

I didn't think I'd made such a deep observation, and it was certainly advice I'd given before. But what I saw as a minor suggestion had a significant effect on the person who received it.

I experienced the same thing that you might; **many of us underestimate what we bring to the table.**

As you track your personal strengths, you'll move past these difficulties. By starting with your reactions (a sense of accomplishment or pride, the desire to have more experiences of the same kind), you'll uncover moments of 'qualitative' accomplishment, which we'll translate into recognizable, job-related skills.

Then, in Chapter 6, you'll see how well your abilities and achievements stack up against those of your competitors (far better than you realize at this point). And if you're not getting the recognition you deserve, all the more reason to make a change!

What advice or expertise do you tend to share as a friend or family member? What do people come to you for? In what circumstances do you feel comfortable jumping in and taking charge? The answers to these questions will reveal situations in which you're seen as an authority. They'll point to abilities you have that others value.

Another tactic is to ask people who know you well what they see as your strengths or your interests. You may be surprised by what they say!

Rewind the tape

Once you make the effort, you'll find plenty of accomplishments that highlight your skill sets, and you'll see how they stand out in the context of your life.

Start by listing 15-25 "trophy moments": things you're pleased to have done in your personal life, your professional life, or any combination of the two.

If you don't have a pad of paper handy, keep a running list on your phone while you go through this exercise. Past accomplishments may occur to you immediately or come to mind over a couple of days. Scribble them on a napkin, the back of a restaurant receipt or in the margin of the box scores--whatever works. Make it easy but get it done.

Try looking back on your life in five-year chunks: your late twenties, your early teens, the past five years, etc.

If you're struggling to come up with 15-25 accomplishments, aim for ten. The key is to start the exercise now and keep at it. It'll be like a large ship: once the propellers get the ship moving, the momentum makes it hard to stop.

I've gone through this a few times myself, and one accomplishment stands out, not for its brilliance, its impact on the world, or quite frankly any relevance outside of my own mind. When you read about it, your reaction may be, "Seriously, Mark, that made your list?" Yet it's something I remember nearly forty years later and I remain proud of it.

In my early teens, I was fascinated by puzzles, games and mazes. I created my own mazes on graph paper, trying to make them as hard as possible. I grew dissatisfied with a one-page maze, and connected nine pages of graph paper together, eventually producing a maze that would take several hours to solve. Okay, hard to believe that makes a blip on my radar. But it highlights several core qualities that remain important to me today, including a commitment to seeing projects through to completion, a fascination with problem-solving and a jump-in-head-first approach to challenges.

You've probably had one or more experiences like that in your past. Give this exercise some time--it will lay the foundation for the work we'll do in the next few chapters. We'll go through the process in stages – identifying strengths and then rethinking them as part of your career-building story. Once you generate your list of moments, we can look deeper to see what they reveal.

Be sure you give this exercise adequate time – it's an essential part of the process.

DIG DEEP

Our next step is to review your list of accomplishments and pick what you consider the top five to ten. Then you'll compose a few sentences about each one, identifying core elements--the underlying traits and skills that brought you a satisfying result.

I want you to write these by hand because countless studies have shown that when you put pen to paper, your brain focuses better, which means more will flow. Don't freeze! If the word "compose" gets in your way, stop thinking of this as a "writing exercise," just see it as jotting some notes down. Take one accomplishment at a time and ask yourself:

* Why did you do it?
* What skills did it require?
* What went well?
* How did you feel about it?
* What made it fun?
* Why did it matter?

Here's how:

The Personal Strengths Tracker

1. List 20-25 accomplishments

2. Choose your top 5-10

3. Write 3-4 sentences about each

4. Identify core elements

5. Look for common threads

LOOK FOR COMMON THREADS

Now look for the common elements that run through all or most of your accomplishments. Did they involve leadership skills? Analysis? Creativity? Organization and planning? Did you operate best alone or as part of a team?

The goal for these sets of paragraphs is to reveal what's compelling for you about each experience, and to help you understand how your accomplishments have guided you to what you're doing now.

Don't worry if this exercise doesn't immediately reveal the specific jobs you should target. The important thing is to highlight the elements of a position that will make you feel fulfilled, challenged and rewarded. Get specific. Are you good with computers? Great at planning events or outings? Gifted at persuading or telling stories? Do you love to coach or show others what you know? If you can complete this simple step, you'll be on your way to finding your true career calling.

Imagine that your current work situation (or the couch you're sitting on) is the equivalent of an overcast, dreary place--in other words, you're not too excited to be there. Now, picture your ideal job as a tropical island on the horizon with beaches and Mai Tais! This process will pull you off your raft adrift in the ocean and onto the speedboat that will take you directly to that island.

You've probably heard that it's "all about the journey," but in your job search, as far as I'm concerned, you need to jump on that speedboat and hit the gas!

Once you've listed your accomplishments and mined them for key information, the next step in your search will be much easier. In Chapter 4, you'll translate your stories into tasks, skills and personality traits that will help identify the right positions and companies for you. Then, with a bit of research and some analysis, you'll be ready to generate your "target list."

DEFINE YOUR IDEAL JOB

"Desire is the key to motivation, but it's determination
and commitment to an unrelenting pursuit of
your goal - a commitment to excellence - that will
enable you to attain the success you seek."

~ MARIO ANDRETTI, INTERNATIONAL MOTOR SPORTS HALL OF FAMER

GREAT NEWS! YOU'RE WELL ON your way. You've wrestled away your negative thoughts and begun to revisit your past for clues about what you do best and enjoy most. Next, we'll complete that review and translate your existing abilities and interests into skills, tasks and preferences you should keep in mind as you search for your ideal job.

WHAT MATTERS MOST?

To be sure you target the industries and positions that suit you best, you'll want to align your job search with your personal values.

You'll be pleasantly surprised to see how your existing abilities and interests translate into marketable skills.

When you consider a possible work situation, ask yourself what priorities steer your decisions, choices and goals. To help you identify pros and cons, read the list below and take note of anything that feels significant.

- **Time:** How important is control of your own schedule? How much leisure time will you need so you can enjoy your days spent at work? Are you willing to sacrifice weekends or evenings in exchange for more money or prestige?
- **Money:** Are you focused on the big bucks? How important is financial compensation compared to location, responsibility, creative freedom or inspiring colleagues?
- **Power:** Do you feel best when you're seen as an expert or influencer? Do you aspire to run a department or division? Are you aiming for the C-suite? How does level of responsibility stack up against other wish-list items like slower pace, less pressure or time with family?
- **Prestige:** Imagine describing your job to a stranger at a cocktail party. What ranks highest on the "proud to share" scale? Get clear on what prestige means to you.

Is it about money? Title and responsibility? Philanthropic or moral contribution?

- **Relationships:** Would you value a position most if it put you in the company of people you enjoy, admire and wish to emulate? Or are you happiest and most productive working on your own?
- **Innovation:** Does the concept of a breakthrough product or service inspire you? Do you love the idea of working on the cutting edge of an industry?
- **Creativity:** Would the chance to use your imagination and creative spirit make you eager to go to work every day?

- **Moral satisfaction:** Are you motivated by the idea of leaving the world better than you found it?

When you align your job search with your core values, you're more likely to target companies and positions you'll be happy in. At the same time, you'll increase your chances of getting hired.

DOWNTIME: LET YOUR INTERESTS FUEL YOUR FUTURE

Apart from documenting your most memorable experiences--the "trophy moments" you turned into core elements of your brand--another way to identify rewarding activities is to examine what you do in your leisure time.

How do you spend your weekends, evenings, holidays and days off? Where do you turn your attention in those moments?

Jog your memory by thinking about events you're pleased to attend, people you choose to spend time with and places you frequent. Books, magazines and newspapers you read. Websites you visit regularly, newsletters you sign up for, types of information you like or share. Where do you volunteer? What hobbies do you pursue? All these will provide clues as you track down your ongoing interests.

REWARDING ACTIVITIES ON THE FIELD AND OFF

To put this all together, you'll generate a list of the interests and skills that bring you the greatest satisfaction--within your sport and outside it. Think of these as one general category: activities you find rewarding.

Through all the changes you experience in your athletic life, your personal life, at work or in the outside world, these activities continue to bring you pleasure. They're a touchstone, a kind of home base you can set out from and return to.

The table below provides a small sample of actions you may have taken in your sport, and corresponding skills in the business world.

In the left column, you'll recognize some that apply to you, and see others that will help you come up with a few of your own. On the right, you'll see phrases you might find in a job description, or hear spoken by a contact, connector or hiring manager. These examples should give you an idea of how to view your accomplishments in the context of a job search or work environment.

In the next few chapters, we'll get more specific about industries and positions. You'll see how this prep work will help you identify companies that are looking for your skills, and organizational cultures in which you'll thrive.

ON THE FIELD AND OFF	
Sports-related activity	**Business-based skill**
Perform in front of a crowd, give interviews, speak to the team	Presenting to senior management and co-workers; public and media relations
Absorb the playbook; implement new strategies	Fast learner; able to ramp up quickly
Motivate teammates	Strong manager; leadership ability
Take direction from coach	Act with full confidence in management
Perform under pressure, adapt to sudden play change	Meet tight deadlines; make decisions in real time; thrive in a fast-paced, high-pressure environment; assess situations quickly; think on your feet; react on the fly
Perform at 100% day and night	High performer; full commitment

MAP YOUR MIND

As you continue generating information for your **Personal Strengths Tracker**, you may need additional assistance in documenting what you've done or visualizing what you want. One technique that helps me is mind mapping. A mind map can help you brainstorm about your job search, and broaden your thinking about your background, strengths and interests.

If you're not familiar with it, mind mapping is a form of visual note-taking that uses not only words but lines, symbols, shapes and pictures. It's a terrific tool for getting ideas and associations into graphic form so you can more easily explore them. It opens the flow for thoughts that may be clogged up...by combining words and visuals in a way that makes perfect sense and is also creative and engaging.

Here's how it works:

> You begin with a central concept (your job search), then capture or "map" all the related thoughts that grow out of it. As ideas pop into your head, you connect them to each other, letting your initial concept branch out into second-level ideas, then third, fourth, etc. until you've exhausted your imagination on the topic. You don't stop to make sense of anything, you don't think about order or structure, you just keep going. When you're done, you'll have a diagram that will help you examine and analyze your ideas about your work experience, your abilities, your interests and your ideal job.

In the mind map at the end of the chapter, the left side lists a few talents typical of former athletes, such as public speaking skills, a strong work ethic, motivational capabilities or comfort in front of the camera. The right side shows some industries that need people with those skills, and (on the bottom right) examples of relevant positions within those industries.

Start considering companies that look for people with your skill set, by creating a mind map where second-level bubbles are company names, third-level are positions at those companies, and fourth-level are actual people in those positions--potential contacts to reach out to and connect with.

I'm a big believer in mind maps, so I encourage you to create many of them while you work through this book. Keep a loose-leaf notebook or legal pad nearby in case you want to diagram as you go.

Your accomplishments, values and leisure activities all contain essential information that will inform your search as you explore possibilities and plan your next career move. The first step of our **Personal Strengths Tracker** used stories from your past to reveal the skills that have given you the greatest satisfaction. The second and third steps guided you through an examination of your values and leisure activities to expand your list of rewarding activities and lay the foundation for developing your brand.

Power play:

If you want more detail about how to use mind maps or how to create more complex ones, visit www.mindmapping.com, or any other of the many websites on mind mapping.

You'll refer often to your skills, values and rewarding activities as you learn my techniques for networking, interviewing and presenting yourself to potential contacts or employers. In the next chapter, you'll turn your personal strengths and interests into a profile on LinkedIn, one of the most powerful tools in today's job search. At the same time, you'll learn how to use the items on your list as keywords when running searches for the industries, companies and positions most aligned with who you are and what you do best.

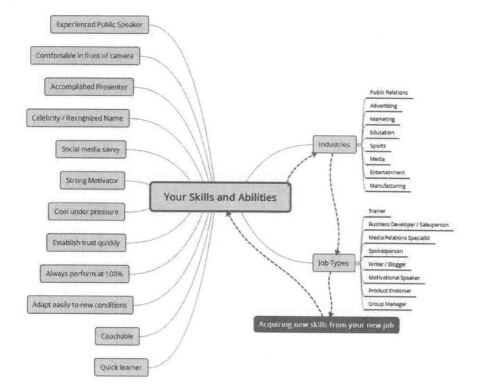

Second Quarter
Identify Your Targets

CHAPTER 5

Show 'Em What You've Got

*"My motto was always to keep swinging. Whether I
was in a slump or feeling badly or having trouble off
the field, the only thing to do was keep swinging."*

~ HANK AARON, MLB HALL OF FAMER, "HAMMERIN' HANK"

To GET RESULTS QUICKLY, YOUR next step will be to establish your presence and jump-start your search on a powerful platform designed to support twenty-first century job searches.

LinkedIn creates networking opportunities that are not available when you apply through a generic job portal. Its cutting-edge research and matching technologies allow you to attract the attention of appropriate recruiters and hiring managers, and reach out to those who would otherwise never know you exist.

With some added imagination and ingenuity (which I'm about to share), you'll be way ahead of the pack of less-informed candidates, and you'll completely transform the way you plan and advance your career.

Important to note: LinkedIn offers several levels of account, from free to a variety of Premium options. I highly recommend you:

1. Spring for one of the Premium choices, at least for the first two months of your search.
2. After that, if you've landed a job and are scaling back your efforts or if you want to minimize expenses, you can drop down to the free version. LinkedIn is continually evolving.
3. At the time of this writing, all the techniques I describe here can be employed by LinkedIn users, but there may be future changes to available functionality. I keep abreast of LinkedIn developments and will post updates and/or workarounds on my site.

Now let's set you up with a LinkedIn account and a profile that gets you noticed.

Creating a compelling profile is much easier than you may think, especially now that your **Personal Strengths Tracker** has revealed the foundations of your personal and professional success. It only takes about an hour, and that hour will provide enormous returns not only for your current job search but also for your long-term career.

Once you've got a profile with the five essential elements below, you'll begin to **show hiring managers who you are and why they need you!** The key to unleashing the power of LinkedIn is to **make yourself visible in the right way.**

A ONE-TWO PUNCH: TELL YOUR STORY WHILE YOU LEARN ABOUT THEIRS

You may be tempted to slow down here and "perfect" your profile, rather than move ahead to research opportunities and make connections. In my experience, a two-pronged approach is best: working back and forth between developing your narrative, and researching industries, companies and jobs.

What you learn as you craft a profile will inform your exploration of potential target companies, and the information you gather as you uncover opportunities will help you describe yourself more effectively. Even if your profile is still a work in progress, it will begin to open doors and set you on the path toward that exciting, ideal job.

If you're a profile perfectionist, you can still go all-out with crafting your narrative--just budget some additional time to get your feet wet on LinkedIn. You won't regret it!

What's in it for them?

Get ready for a total game-changer: As you conduct your job search, always put yourself in the shoes of the person reading your profile. Anticipate their needs, objections and concerns--determine what will attract them or turn them away.

You may already have a LinkedIn account and be reasonably well- connected. Maybe you've added contacts, posted information about yourself, and even acquired endorsements or recommendations.

This does NOT mean you're maximizing the power of LinkedIn.

> **Power play:**
>
> ALWAYS put yourself in the shoes of the person viewing your profile. Ask yourself what's in it for them, and make the answer perfectly clear to your reader.

Did you know that your profile can turn potential employers away?

LinkedIn has become THE destination for hiring managers and recruiters, whether they're looking for candidates who are active, "passive" (i.e., happy enough in their current position and unaware of more fulfilling options) or just building networks.

To this day I consider it an essential resource as I conduct searches on behalf of my executive search clients. If you're not on LinkedIn, I'm unlikely to submit you for any role I'm representing, and most executive recruiters will feel the same.

LinkedIn is where proactive users make their presence known and lay the groundwork for career moves down the road.

But as with any powerful tool, you need to know how to use it…

Your LinkedIn profile: five essential elements

When a hiring manager, recruiter, or anyone else conducts a LinkedIn search or receives an invitation to connect, they immediately see a Photo, Job Title, Geographic Location and Workplace.

If any one of these offers a reason to reject you, chances are they will. But if you have a professional-looking picture, a compelling title, and a clear indication of where you work (or have worked), they'll likely move on to your full profile and accept your invitation once you send it (more on that later).

Essential Element 1: Your photo

Make sure you look presentable and appropriate for your industry. And remember, *you* are the subject of the photo. Not your cat, your car or someone else's arm. I suggest you look at other profiles to get a feel for which types of photos, poses, backgrounds, lighting, etc. work best for someone in your area of interest. If you're targeting finance, then clearly that means a suit for men, and a similar professional outfit for women. If you're considering roles in IT or advertising, a more casual look is fine but keep it professional. Appearances truly matter!

Essential Element 2: Your job "title"

LinkedIn uses *job title* to refer to what you put in the "title" slot of your profile. If you don't enter your own information, LinkedIn will autofill your title (based on your experience section) unless you edit the title slot yourself, so it's up to you to use this section to your best advantage.

You don't have to list the title your employer has given you or a position you recently held. Come up with something intriguing that captures the essence of what you do. You can choose catchier words like "specialist" or "strategist." Instead of "Financial Planner for Bank of America," try "Financial Services Strategist."

Follow up on that first title with other ones like "Fixed Income Product Specialist," "Media Relations Expert" or "Business Development Specialist." A more descriptive title gives the reader a better understanding of the tasks you'll be able to perform.

You don't have to name your company in the title slot, since it appears in the following line where you list your workplace. So be inventive (while still being accurate) and use your title to spark interest.

LinkedIn allows 120 characters for your title, use them well!

Essential Element 3: Your current workplace

Do not omit this! Including a workplace is essential because it establishes that you're either a current employee, a recently retired athlete, a student or a candidate in transition. If you're in transition, you can mention volunteering, training or classes you're enrolled in.

Essential Element 4: Your summary statement

Can you imagine submitting a resume with a big chunk of your work experience missing? Or sending a cover letter without an introductory paragraph? That's what your LinkedIn profile looks like when you neglect your summary statement.

Most recruiters and hiring managers won't give your profile a second thought if you leave out your summary--the dreaded section of your profile where you need to write about yourself and summarize your skills and accomplishments. It's the section most people either nail or totally fail at, and the most important one for hiring managers.

The people you want to connect with will take the time to read this section, and they'll judge you by what they find there. It's a reflection of how you value yourself and how much effort you've put into marketing your brand.

Your summary statement is your brand

You shouldn't let this scare you, but you must take the steps to get your profile primed and ready to go! The key to nailing the summary statement is to make it *a simple, clear description of who you are, what you do and what you bring to a business or organization.*

Don't get caught up writing out every detail of your work experience or every task you've ever undertaken. Make sure you're direct and to the point, and really highlight who you are as a potential employee.

This is almost like having an initial conversation with a hiring manager or recruiter. So be genuine, keep it concise and let people know what you're looking for.

Can you describe an accomplishment or a moment that allowed you to shine? Are there sales numbers to document how much you contributed to revenue growth in a single quarter? This is the kind of measurable success you'll want to point out.

Make it clear that you're a team player, that you have a solid work ethic. If you think you're a top-notch leader who does well in fast-paced environments...say so! While you don't want to sound generic, you need to highlight what makes you tick and how you work best in professional settings.

As you define and create your presence on LinkedIn, keep referring to your **Personal Strengths Tracker** and use that information to generate and support the elements of your profile.

Go those extra yards

When it comes to your summary statement, a little extra effort will go a very long way, so take the steps below to be sure you're putting your best foot forward.

Craft it. Many people simply write down everything they've ever done, or cut and paste their resume into their summary statement. That's not an effective strategy. Think of your summary statement as your "chef's specialties" and not a list of everything on the menu! It's a great way to spoon-feed your readers so they see the tasks you've performed and the skills you possess in light of what their organization needs.

Beware of focusing too much on the past instead of the future: if you no longer want to balance P&L statements, don't highlight that part of your experience--it will only get you noticed by those who want P&L statements balanced. Or if you have a reputation for being comfortable speaking in front of a crowd, don't highlight your ability to balance a budget when targeting a public relations position.

Edit it. When you've got a rough draft of your summary statement, edit it! Make sure it tells a coherent story that doesn't ramble or digress. Review it for grammar, spelling and punctuation (even if you're not applying for a writing or communications position, incorrect sentences or misspelled words can be deal-breakers).

If this is outside your wheelhouse, get a helpful friend or relative to give it a once-over. Or hire an editor. It's only a page or so, but it forms the basis of your LinkedIn strategy.

Proof it. After writing and editing comes proofreading. This is about catching glitches: typos, missing words, odd spacing--those little mishaps that make big statements about your level of commitment and attention to detail. Studies have shown that we're never well-equipped to proof our own writing--we see what we intended to write, not what's on the page. So once again, have someone else check your work.

Publish it. Now post your summary statement on your LinkedIn page! It doesn't have to be perfect. You'll continue to modify it as you conduct your research and refine your target list. As long as it describes you accurately, in engaging language and without glaring mistakes, it will set you up well and get you noticed.

Bottom line: go those extra yards to show hiring managers and key influencers that you're worth an initial conversation. If you follow the strategy I've outlined so far, chances are people will reach out to you and try to sell you on working for their company.

It's all in how you position yourself and make yourself known on the greatest professional platform around!

Essential Element 5: Get Recommendations

Another surefire way to attract and maintain the attention of decision-makers is through LinkedIn recommendations. You want to get these from a cross-section of professionals and key influencers in both the athletic world and the industry you're targeting.

Please note that I didn't say "endorsements." On LinkedIn, people can endorse you by simply clicking on those skills you've listed for yourself. Often, they do this to appear on your feed and have your profile appear on theirs. In my opinion, endorsements are too easy to give and receive and therefore say nothing about you.

The best tactic for getting recommendations is to look through your list of LinkedIn connections and choose six to eight to reach out to with that

> **Power play:**
>
> For instructions on creating a printed list of your LinkedIn connections for easy reference, see Chapter 7.

request. Make sure to select people senior in their field, so others will be impressed that they were willing to vouch for you. Of course, if your former coach or manager is not senior, you still want them to contribute.

Since nearly everyone is too busy to craft language on your behalf, send them a template to show what you'd like them to include in your recommendation.

For example, your former coach or manager could say:

Aaron was one of the finest athletes I've ever coached, not simply because of his athletic skills but because he brought an incredible work ethic to the field every day. He demonstrated leadership qualities far above what others have at that stage of their careers. His ability to earn the respect of fellow teammates and coaching staff and his patience when training others with less experience set him apart.

He will continue to be a strong leader, able to manage a group and train its members with ease. His ability to handle pressure in a time-sensitive environment and his insistence on performing at the top of his game at all times will make him a tremendous addition to any company.

Here's another example from somebody you used to work for or someone in the industry you're targeting:

Stephanie is one of the brightest, most enthusiastic and positive people I've ever known. Her work ethic is extraordinary: she demonstrates coolness under fire but brings a necessary edge when needed. She has consistently proven herself comfortable and effective in front of a camera or on stage. Without a doubt, she can perform admirably in a media relations environment.

I urge any company looking to increase their standing within their industry to strongly consider adding Stephanie to their team, and I'm more than happy to speak with anyone directly about her and her tremendous skill set.

Not bad, eh?

There are plenty of examples I could list, but a better option for you is to explore LinkedIn to see how others are being recommended. When you see language that fits the position you're targeting, feel free to adapt it for your templates and requests.

One caveat: Do not recommend someone who is recommending you. It will be clear to the reader of your profile that the two of you were swapping a favor.

> **Power play:**
>
> Strong recommendations are extremely effective in getting you noticed and hired.

Getting recommendations is a very important step!

It's worth every minute you invest to add stellar recommendations to your increasingly impressive LinkedIn profile.

HOW TO ANSWER: *"WHAT DO YOU DO?"*

You're at a cocktail party, a barbecue or family gathering, and at some point (or on several occasions), a person comes up to you and asks: **"So... what do you do?"** Or maybe: "What do you do for a living? Who do you work for? What industry are you in?" You probably don't realize it, but people ask you this every day in a number of ways and in a variety of settings. It's almost always the initial question from a person you meet for the first time.

Having a great answer ready is a terrific way to break the ice, find out who they know and, most important, learn what opportunities they can offer. But chances are you're missing out on the chance to score big here-- to tell them who you are, what you want to do, and how they can help.

When someone asks what you do, your immediate response may be: "I'm an ex-basketball player with the Chicago Bulls"; "I'm doing business development for my friend's company"; "I'm a litigation attorney at a medium-sized law firm"; or "I work as a portfolio manager in financial services." Even worse: "I dunno, not much, I'm sort of between jobs." (Eeek!)

Then you'll probably ask what *they* do for a living, and the two of you will go back and forth before you move on to other topics of conversation. Or you'll turn your attention to the baseball game on TV, to other guests playing pool, to flipping the burgers or whatever. Big mistake!

The *"What do you do?"* question is an extremely valuable and time-sensitive opportunity to enhance your network and turbo-charge your job search. Instead of answering with a job title, describe your interests and your expertise. It's much more engaging! You'll win your listener's attention immediately, and from there you can turn the situation to your advantage.

Let's say Troy asks: "Sofia, what do you do for a living?"

Instead of simply stating, "I'm a financial advisor," she might say: "For the past 15 years I've been providing financial strategies and easy-to-understand investment solutions to people who are either too busy to manage their own funds, or don't have their finger on the pulse of the market like I do. I'm looking to speak with savvy professionals who recognize the value of having a financial strategist like myself to partner with in managing their finances."

But she shouldn't stop there...

Sofia should continue: "Is there anyone you know of who might benefit from a quick chat about my services? Or do you have any advice on how I might best grow my network in that area?"

Now Troy is much more likely to be intrigued, and say: "Interesting... tell me more about those strategies..." or "Actually, my good friend Cooper has been looking for a capable financial manager. He's right over here, let me introduce you to him..."

If you're a former athlete transitioning into the business world, instead of saying, "I used to play rugby for the USA Women's National Team," focus on how that experience will translate into the job you'd love to have. "As captain of the Women's National Team, I needed leadership skills and a strong work ethic to deliver a consistent, high-level performance every day. I'm looking to combine that experience with my finance education and bring those skills and traits to a real estate development firm." And continue with, "What advice would you have for me as I make that transition? Is there anyone in your network you'd suggest I meet with?"

Your conversation partner will very likely offer advice, and, more important, consider introducing you to key influencers in real estate development. Best of all, if one of those influencers is in the room, you may get an introduction right away, and can strike up a conversation using the techniques you're learning in this book. You'll be miles ahead of where you were before you came to the event!

Sharing the right information is a critical part of securing a job lead. And don't pivot away too quickly! Don't immediately ask them what *they* do, right after your initial statement (you'll get there eventually). Instead, ask them to think of people they know who work in the field you want to enter.

ASK FOR ADVICE AND YOU'LL RECEIVE IT -- GUARANTEED!

If you ask for a job or offer your resume, people will stop listening to whatever you're saying. Also guaranteed! Even worse, they may run screaming, check their watch or announce that they need another drink. Keep them engaged! Don't shift the focus away from yourself. Ask for a referral or introduction to someone in their network. That person will probably know someone who knows someone who can get you a conversation with another someone at the company you want to join.

Having your answers ready and using these techniques will expand your network dramatically

How do you prepare for these "what do you do" moments? Practice! Take the core of your story (from your accomplishments and LinkedIn profile) and turn it into a brief statement of your value proposition. Ten seconds is all you need and probably all you'll get to make that first impression.

Your value proposition in ten seconds or less

Let's face it: people are busy. They've got their own problems, their own goals, their own agendas. If you're going to win them over and turn them into an ally or advocate, you've got to do it fast! Show them right away why they should give you their attention. Bait the hook and dangle it--then, once they bite, you can reel them in more slowly.

Take your answer to *"What do you do?"* and distill it down to its most concentrated form. Aim for 2-3 sentences that are general enough to pique most people's interest. Don't mention specifics yet--you'll add details as you continue to chat. Then prepare and rehearse answers to a handful of follow-up questions so you can elaborate and weave in bits of carefully-calculated information, dropped into the conversation in an off-handed, "spontaneous" way!

Defense as offense: don't hand over your resume... yet!

How many times have you been in a meeting, professional event or casual environment, when someone says to you, "Hey, did you bring a copy of your resume? I'd love to see your resume... Send me your resume...I'll float your resume around my office..."

Do not send your resume!

I forbid you to send it. Tell them you're still working on it...that you'll send it a week from now, a month from now, ten years from now, whenever. But don't send it to them.

Instead, offer to send them a LinkedIn connection request and, at the very least, email them the link to your profile. Include your LinkedIn profile link in your email signature, and title it "My LinkedIn Profile" instead of the actual link address.

Your goal (and your <u>only</u> goal here) is to arrange a meeting, schedule a phone call, or promote yourself in any other manner than sending your resume.

Why? Because your resume is a two-dimensional representation of you. It doesn't showcase your talent or make clear what's unique about you. When people ask for a resume, they're looking for the lazy solution.

> **Coach says:**
>
> Include your LinkedIn profile link in your email signature. Title it "My LinkedIn Profile."

It's a way to sound helpful while avoiding doing anything to help you.

Instead of sending your resume, push for an informal meeting.

Say, "Look, I'd love to send you my resume but, in the meantime, why don't I swing by your office? We can have a cup of coffee and explore how my network might help yours, or how my skill set might be useful to your organization." Something like that.

Push for the meeting and then, during that informal conversation, lay out your value proposition; show the person, in a general way, what you're about, and let him know you're asking for his advice. "Hey, what does your company look for?" Or "Do you know of other companies that might need someone with my expertise?" Or even very simply: "This is what I bring to the table. What kind of ideas would you have for me? What kind of advice can you give?"

That just might spark him to say, "Would you ever consider working for us? We might have some openings here." And then you answer, "Absolutely. Let's talk more about what you're looking for." From there, your new connector may say, "Let me set up a call or a meeting," and you're on your way to sitting down with key influencers, decision makers, hiring managers or Human Resources.

The point I'm making is that **the resume is your last line of attack, not your first**. It's what they'll ask for later in the process, after you've made a great first and second impression. Your resume is something to reference but not your lead-in. Tell your story, engage your audience, then later you can send them the script.

Alright...you still need a resume

By now you understand that sending out resumes is not the answer. You can submit hundreds of them and never get anywhere; they'll just get lost in the abyss of the internet.

Instead, focus on expanding your professional network, having casual conversations and earning meetings that lead to interviews and offers.

Still, despite the fact that resumes can cause job-seeker despair, they're a necessary evil. And I use the word evil because you can ask 100 people for their opinion about your resume and you'll get 150 different answers. Everybody's got their ideas on how a resume should look, including me.

Here's my advice: keep it short and to the point. No one cares that you invented the Betamax back in 1812. I promise you. They don't. They want to see capabilities you can bring to their environment and understand how you can apply your expertise to hit a home run for their team. Focus on the accomplishments and skills you can leverage in the types of positions you want to go after.

Getting your resume right

When the time comes to provide your resume, you want it to do its job. In other words, you want it to tell the story you've chosen to tell and not sound like you cribbed it off the internet. You want it to be the one chosen for an interview…the one that rises to the top of the pile!

Just as with your LinkedIn summary, you need a resume that *compels* people to meet you. Hiring managers typically glance at a resume for six or seven seconds and often decide based on that initial impression.

Use this checklist to capture their attention immediately and intrigue them enough to continue reading.

1) **Summary Statement**: Start with 2-3 sentences that showcase your top-line skills and expertise. You can highlight aspects of your current job, but don't emphasize skills you no longer want to use or tasks you feel you've moved beyond. Avoid words you'd never say in conversation…you'll get more ridicule than praise if you jam your summary full of corporate speak.

2) **Body:** Next, include your greatest hits: the accomplishments you want to be remembered for, not everything you did at each company where you worked. People don't care what you've done in the past (either positive or negative) unless it will directly impact them going forward. Think like your reader!

3) **Education**: Your degrees, and the dates when you received them, are important, along with any impressive awards conferred on you during that time. But unless you recently graduated and the classes you took are relevant to the position you're seeking, do not include a list of them. Introduction to Basic Economics or Solving Sudoku 201 will not impress anyone (other than Sudoku enthusiasts). Make sure you place your education *under* your experience, as work history is what hiring managers focus on most.

4) **Interests**: If you feel obligated to announce your interests, **list only those that are unique and compelling**! Meaning, don't include: reading, writing, walking or breathing! If you're into jiu-jitsu, glass blowing, or reciting Shakespeare, I want to hear more… and so might the hiring manager, but if your hobbies are nothing out of the ordinary, save the white space.

Don't procrastinate. As you get closer to receiving an offer, somebody may insist you send your resume, so don't put off cleaning it up. After all, in addition to your LinkedIn profile, this is the document many will refer to both before and after you meet them.

Okay. You're set up on LinkedIn. You've got your ten-second pitch. You've updated your resume and prepared a well-crafted and well-rehearsed answer to *What do you do?* Later, in chapter 10, I'll show you how to expand and make much more of your presence on LinkedIn, but right now I want to get you a target list. Let's play ball!

CHAPTER 6

CALL THE SHOTS

"For the eighteen months after I retired,
all I did was surf the internet
without knowing what I was really looking for..."

~ THEOREN FLEURY, NHL ALL-STAR, OLYMPIAN

FINDING YOUR IDEAL JOB ISN'T quick and easy, but you've gotten through the toughest part!

You've reviewed your accomplishments, noted your values and interests, and solidified your understanding of what you have to offer, then translated that information into short and longer versions of your "story."

Now you'll create a list of positions that sound appealing and companies you think you'd be happy to work for. From here on, the process should become a lot more fun.

YOUR TARGET LIST: INDUSTRIES, COMPANIES AND JOBS

I'm about to show you how to use LinkedIn to gain insight into positions you can excel at and enjoy. But first, let's capture what immediately comes to mind. Without thinking hard, jot down the types of jobs you feel drawn to or curious about. What would you do if all options were open? If you followed your instincts or your passions? If you knew for certain you'd succeed? You might surprise yourself with industries you haven't focused on or positions you've never considered. Fundraising? Hospitality? Education? Information Technology?

For more inspiration, you can conduct online searches about fields you want to investigate. Be attentive to your reactions whenever you read or hear about companies or jobs.

When you see an interview on television or learn about a product breakthrough or marketing triumph, or when a friend describes their current or previous work experience, what piques your interest? What makes you curious, envious or impressed? When do you think, "That sounds cool!" or "I bet I'd like to do that!"

One place to start is with a recent study of "best places to work." Forbes puts out a yearly list,[3] as do Fortune, Business Insider, Glass Door and many others.

You can think in terms of industries, and then search for organizations within the ones that appeal. The list below presents 16 "Career Clusters" with explanations of what they entail and the skills they require.

Don't worry if nothing jumps out at you right away. As you follow my system for working with LinkedIn, you'll get ideas that will direct your research and, at the same time, you may be prompted to add to or modify your profile, resume and ten-second pitch.

The goal here is to put together a list of 40-50 companies you either know well or have heard great things about.

That list will grow as you work through the next few chapters, but a simple math equation shows that 40+ companies and five or so positions will lead you to 200 +/- jobs that could be a great fit for you.

At any given time, at least 10-20 of those jobs are being actively recruited for, whether online (unlikely) or under the radar (very likely), or the company is looking at candidates for upcoming needs. What better way to land your ideal job than to proactively reach out to hiring managers directly involved with those openings?

---

[3] [https://www.forbes.com/sites/jeffkauflin/2016/12/07/the-best-places-to-work-in-2017/#3c2ebd638b16]

The 16 Career Clusters[4]

Agriculture, Food & Natural Resources: The production, processing, marketing, distribution, financing, and development of agricultural commodities and resources including food, fiber, wood products, natural resources, horticulture, and other plant and animal products/resources.

Architecture and Construction: Careers in designing, planning, managing, building and maintaining the built environment.

Arts, AV Technology & Communications: Designing, producing, exhibiting, performing, writing, and publishing multimedia content including visual and performing arts and design, journalism, and entertainment services.

Business Management and Administration: Business Management and Administration careers encompass planning, organizing, directing and evaluating business functions essential to efficient and productive business operations. Business Management and Administration career opportunities are available in every sector of the economy.

Education & Training: Planning, managing and providing education and training services, and related learning support services.

Finance: Planning, services for financial and investment planning, banking, insurance, and business financial management.

Government & Public Administration: Executing governmental functions to include Governance; National Security; Foreign Service; Planning; Revenue and Taxation; Regulation; and Management and Administration at the local, state, and federal levels.

---

[4] Reprinted with permission from *National Association of State Directors of Career Technical Education Consortium (NASDCTEc)*

Health Science: Planning, managing, and providing therapeutic services, diagnostic services, health informatics, support services, and biotechnology research and development.

Hospitality & Tourism: Hospitality & Tourism encompasses the management, marketing and operations of restaurants and other food services, lodging, attractions, recreation events and travel related services.

Human Services: Preparing individuals for employment in career pathways that relate to families and human needs.

Information Technology: Building linkages in IT occupations framework: For entry level, technical, and professional careers related to the design, development, support and management of hardware, software, multimedia, and systems integration services.

Law, Public Safety, Corrections & Security: Planning, managing, and providing legal, public safety, protective services and homeland security, including professional and technical support services.

Manufacturing: Planning, managing and performing the processing of materials into intermediate or final products and related professional and technical support activities such as production planning and control, maintenance and manufacturing/process engineering.

Marketing, Sales & Service: Planning, managing, and performing marketing activities to reach organizational objectives.

Science, Technology, Engineering & Mathematics: Planning, managing, and providing scientific research and professional and technical services (e.g., physical science, social science, engineering) including laboratory and testing services, and research and development services.

Transportation, Distribution & Logistics: Planning, management, and movement of people, materials, and goods by road, pipeline, air, rail and water and related professional and technical support services such as transportation infrastructure planning and management, logistics services, mobile equipment and facility maintenance.

Unleash the power of LinkedIn

One of the many benefits of a LinkedIn account is the ability to conduct extensive research on those jobs and companies that will make up your target list. It's very simple. Just follow the steps below:

1. In the search box near the top of the home page, type in the name of a company you think you'd like to work for, for example: Wells Fargo.
2. Without hitting "enter," look through the items in the drop-down until you see "Company Page."
3. Open the company page to get a ton of company-specific information, such as a breakdown of company functions, total number of employees, recent hires, and notable alumni, along with open jobs and pages for similar companies.
4. Follow these leads to learn more about who they've been hiring, see open job searches, etc.
5. Make note of details you'd like to follow up on in your next LinkedIn research session.
6. See who at Wells Fargo is already in your network or just a few degrees away! Then visit their personal profiles to learn (in detail) about what they actually do.
7. You can also run specific key word searches to find out which employees at Wells Fargo may have business development, public speaking, equity analysis, or even C++ programming in their

backgrounds, and take a deeper dive into how they use those skills at their job.

8. To keep track of all the information you gather on LinkedIn, it's helpful to have a simple tracking and management system. In the next chapter, I'll show you my method and give you instructions for applying it.

Suppose I've looked through the industry list and decided that Marketing sounds like it could be a good choice for me. I've done some preliminary research (or heard from a friend) about *XYZ Marketing Solutions.* They've won several awards for their recent campaigns and I like the way employees talk about the company culture. I want to know what it's like to work in XYZ's marketing department. I type "XYZ Marketing Solutions" in LinkedIn's search box. Then I click the arrow for the drop-down box and look for "Company Page."

Here I find out that they specialize in brand management and digital media, have 150 employees and have hired three Business Developers this year. I make note of their job posting for a Business Development Associate and capture the names of two people currently holding that position: Jeremy and Laura.

I also notice a more senior member of the department, Luke, who's a second-degree connection, through a buddy of mine from college. Now I'll see what Jeremy and Laura do

> **Power play:**
>
> LinkedIn shows you which employees are in your network, and then allows you to review their personal profiles and learn more about what they actually do.

for XYZ and how they describe their professional experience. Then I'll either reach out to my buddy to make an introduction to Luke, or I'll send an invitation to Luke directly.

Important Note: Job titles can be misleading! Many functions are called different things in different organizations. The tasks and responsibilities for a role at one company may not be the same as those for the same position at another.

Most profiles include details about what the person does as well as their title, so I recommend you study a number of profiles for any given position to see how they list or describe the tasks and different aspects of their job.

Typically, people list job functions in one of the following orders: how often they perform them, the importance of the function or their level of interest in it. This will give you an overall feel for what it's like to work in that job for that company.

LinkedIn is a place where professionals describe what they do and how they do it. When you're researching, experiment with search parameters by entering both relevant and random key words into the LinkedIn search bar. "Equity analyst Ukrainian" will show you how people leverage language skills in the financial arena. "Writer public speaker" lets you see the many ways in which those types of expertise can be applied. You'll also notice attributes that tend to be listed together. You might find you've forgotten to mention some skills of your own!

You'll soon find that you can spend hours at a time on LinkedIn, researching what people do, what companies are about, and the types of jobs they tend to offer. All this will contribute to the ongoing development of your target list and the refinement of your story.

Remember to work back and forth between your **Personal Strengths Tracker** and the results of your LinkedIn research. And don't forget to align your search with your values and leisure activities.

> **Foul!**
>
> Job titles can be misleading! Many functions are called different things in different organizations.

For example, if reviewing how you spend your spare time reminds you how much you love to travel, hold that thought as you learn about industries or companies and investigate opportunities.

Playbook

One of my clients--a financial modeling analyst--had spent several months targeting financial services companies, sending resumes and filling out applications online without getting a single bite. He'd grown frustrated and depressed, wondering why nobody could see how strong a hire he'd be.

As soon as he began my coaching program, we got started tracking his strengths and compiling his target list. Although he had tremendous analytical skills, it turned out he also had a strong interest and understanding of the travel industry, and had travelled extensively throughout his career and personal life.

After six weeks of employing the WIN AGAIN playbook, he joined the financial modeling team at Expedia. Once he understood that his accomplishments and interests would guide him towards his dream job, he created a target list that focused on the travel industry, and was quickly hired into a job he'd never considered before.

Go after the jobs you want, not what the market feeds you

Every day millions of people wake up, pour themselves coffee, turn on their computers, and scour online job boards, corporate websites or LinkedIn. Those millions of people are doing it all wrong! They're reacting to what the job market feeds them instead of being proactive and going after the positions they want.

It doesn't matter if the company is actively hiring for your position right now.

Here's the single best piece of advice I can give, the one shift that can put you in the top two percent of job seekers: **Be Proactive, Not Reactive!**

You'd think this would be common knowledge among people looking for work, but most have no idea what a difference it makes. As a result, 98% of job seekers make things harder, not easier on themselves. They sit at their desk or lie on their couch with their laptop open, eyes glazed over, their future hanging on the hope that someone will fall in love with the resume they've submitted.

Then they wait. And wait. And eventually many stop waiting because, quite frankly, they've lost all motivation. That hope for a successful future is left hanging in internet limbo.

Don't waste your time trying to fit your background into descriptions you see online. The truth is, most positions on corporate websites have already been filled by the time you read about them: they've been uploaded only to satisfy federal guidelines and corporate policy. It's a depressing reality for many, but it doesn't have to be yours.

If you want the job you deserve, you need to go get it!

And the way to do that is through targeted search and proactive networking.

This scene plays out in corporate America every day:

Frank tells his manager Caroline he's leaving for another firm and gives her his two weeks' notice!

Caroline panics--even if just a little, wondering how she'll replace Frank by the time his notice period ends. The first thing she does is look in her desk drawer for resumes of people she's previously met or spoken with or those who've been referred to her. (We'd like to think you're at the top of this pile, but in most cases, nobody in the drawer is appropriate.) She then reaches out to her team, asking if they know anyone who would be a good fit. Jim has a neighbor who rides the train with a guy who's heard of a woman named Jennifer who's got the right background. (Yes, this is how it often goes!) Caroline invites Jennifer for a set of interviews and the team is excited about hiring her, as is Caroline.

Next, Caroline calls Human Resources to say she wants to hire Jennifer. But HR says, "Whoa, Caroline, not so fast. You need to put together a job description, post the position on the company website for at least two weeks and interview a diverse slate of candidates." Caroline is not enthusiastic about making this extra effort as she's perfectly happy with Jennifer, but she complies with HR policy.

She posts a description that's seen by hundreds of potential candidates who think, "Wow--I'm perfect for this job!" or "I can do this job, even though I don't have programming experience." (Sound familiar?) Human Resources whittles down the massive influx of resumes and applications, and sends Caroline several for review. Caroline holds firm: she still wants Jennifer. She may interview a couple of candidates to satisfy company guidelines or HR, or she may simply move forward and offer Jennifer the position.

Bottom line: all those applicants who thought they had a shot at the position had no idea it had already been filled by the time they saw the posting. While this is not the case for every job listed, it happens often enough to reduce your already low odds of landing a job by applying online.

THE HIDDEN JOB MARKET

In every company, people get hired under the radar--at least 80% of open positions are filled through networking. So rather than wasting your energy trying to look like the ideal candidate for a non-existent job or a job you're settling for, invest 80%+ of your time developing and maintaining professional contacts.

Identify the positions you want, or the companies you want to be part of, then connect with the key influencers, hiring managers, decision-makers and human resources professionals who are directly associated with those jobs. Sending them a personalized invitation on LinkedIn will lead to phone conversations or casual coffee meetings, followed by interviews, and eventually an offer for a position you'll love. It's not only possible, it happens every single day.

If you sit and wait for the right job to present itself, you'll need a boatload of good luck, and even with that you'll be waiting a very long time. The key is to be proactive by examining your accomplishments, values and interests to generate an accurate, engaging story about yourself and what you offer. When you use that information to fuel your research on LinkedIn, you end up with a target list of jobs to go after and a better sense of how to position yourself for those jobs.

If you're reading this, you've probably already completed those steps. If not, go back and work your way to this point. We're about to kick things up and get you talking to the people that count!

HALFTIME HIGHLIGHTS

We've covered a lot of ground and we're about to launch into the second half of this program, where you'll turn your preparation and hard work into victory!

The hardest part of this process is behind you. Ahead are the two primary plays of job transition and career building: networking and interviewing. In the coming chapters, I'll be giving you simple, step-by-step instructions for networking and interviewing like a champ, but first let's review all you've accomplished so far.

* If you started this book feeling that your best days were behind you, you understand now that you've still got a big game to play, and that your experience as an athlete has set you up to identify and go after the job that will bring you the greatest satisfaction in this next phase of your professional life.

- You've taken control of your mindset and dispensed with the mistaken notions that you're too old, not qualified, lacking connections, unable to compete or at the mercy of an uncooperative job market.
- Using the Personal Strengths Tracker, you assessed your abilities and then aligned them with your core values and interests. You created a list of "trophy moments," your proudest accomplishments within and outside of your sport, then reworked them into elements of your career-building story.
- You translated your proudest accomplishments and most rewarding experiences into the tasks, skills and personality traits that form the basis of your brand.
- With a greater understanding of what makes you tick--tasks you enjoy, people you work well with, environments in which you thrive--you began to identify industries, companies and positions most likely to be a good fit.
- You were introduced to and encouraged to make the most of the extraordinary power of LinkedIn, the premiere site for showcasing and finding professional talent. I showed you how to work back and forth between fine-tuning your LinkedIn profile and identifying targets for your search.
- You worked through a series of simple steps for generating a LinkedIn profile that highlights your expertise and gets you noticed by the right people: photo, job title, geographic location, current workplace, summary statement and recommendations.
- We tackled the (often-intimidating) summary statement--the essence of your brand--and broke it down into manageable, common-sense components.
- You crafted a ten-second pitch to grab attention immediately and make clear who you are and what you bring to the table.
- You got yourself ready to answer the inevitable question: *"What do you do?"*

- We dealt with the controversial topic of resumes, acknowledging that a resume is a necessary evil, and you worked through my checklist to be sure your resume is doing its job.

- You learned to present yourself to hiring managers, contacts and potential employers as the solution to their problems and a major asset to their team.

- You created a target list of industries, companies and positions most likely to bring out the best in you and keep you focused, productive, happy and well-rewarded.

- To help you further develop your target list, I taught you techniques for researching people and positions so you can continually expand your network.

- You know how to refine your story, expand your target list and focus on what you want, not what the market feeds you.

- You know that the most practical approach is to dream big and go after your ideal job.

Are you ready for the Second Half?

In the upcoming chapters, I'll show you how to become an all-star networker and gold-medal interviewer. These two skills are a formidable combination because the goal of networking is to drive interviews, and successful interviews lead to more targeted networking as well as to jobs!

Third Quarter
Grow Your Network

CHAPTER 7

BUILD YOUR NETWORK

"You miss one hundred percent of the shots you don't take."

~ WAYNE GRETZKY, NHL HALL OF FAMER, "THE GREAT ONE"

BY NOW YOU'VE GOT A greatly-improved LinkedIn profile with a professional-looking photo, attention-grabbing title, a concise, well-thought-out summary statement and impressive recommendations. It's essential to set yourself up on LinkedIn because in today's job market, it's all about the network!

Resumes are much less central to the process these days, in large part because we've all learned to look online when deciding where to invest our dollars and our trust. The authority you establish and the reputation you build on LinkedIn will go a long way toward encouraging people to connect and engage with you.

Studies show that a majority of positions (some say more than 80%) are filled by some degree of networking. To see how that works, let's reverse-engineer the process.

BREAK IT DOWN: NETWORKING REVERSE-ENGINEERED

To land a job you really want, you need to get an offer. An offer generally follows a series of interviews, which usually results from some informal meetings, which grew out of more casual interactions--and those are often triggered by LinkedIn invitations or other ways of connecting and building a network.

Looked at from that angle, when you send invitations on LinkedIn, you're initiating professional relationships, with the goal of moving toward your ideal job.

The most effective way to establish relationships is to schedule low-key, informal meetings, where you and another person exchange information and advice, and explore how you can help each other by expanding or merging your networks. When you meet face-to-face, you ask intelligent questions, you seek their advice and you make them feel important, because they are!

In the course of the conversation, you find an opportunity to describe what you can contribute, as in, "I've got 20 years' experience increasing the bottom line of companies. I've been successful at expanding visibility in the marketplace and I'm looking to bring my advertising and marketing expertise to smaller companies and startups. What do you think, Nina... is there anyone you'd recommend I speak to...at a company other than yours?"

Notice how "a company other than yours," takes the pressure off Nina because you're not asking her to help you get hired into her organization. At the same time, this starts her thinking: "What about us? This guy is smart, experienced and personable--he'd be a great addition to our team..." And now your casual meeting has become almost an interview, but it's not an interview, because there are no expectations--you're relaxed, just chewing the fat.

Before you say goodbye, Nina may well add, "You know, I'd be happy to present you to our HR department or talk to our head of marketing about you." Or she may say nothing, but then mention you to key decision makers, influencers or hiring managers, either right away or in the future.

Companies love internal referrals because they come from someone who understands the organization and its culture, and knows what it takes to succeed there. When you get recommended by a current employee, your chances of becoming a candidate skyrocket!

GET THE BALL ROLLING RIGHT AWAY

In my opinion, the number one secret to successful job searching is creating and maintaining professional relationships with key influencers, decision-makers and hiring managers in the industry, or people holding the positions you've decided to target.

That's why, with the *WIN AGAIN* playbook, you'll invest over 80% of your job-searching time in networking, especially using LinkedIn. I recommend sending 20-50 invitations to carefully selected people *every day*. You'll soon see how easy it is to make these connections, even if you're not comfortable introducing yourself to new people. It's quick, it's easy and it pays off big-time.

Most of us are comfortable contacting friends and close colleagues but hesitate to approach senior-level professionals. On LinkedIn, you can establish relationships with people you would otherwise never have access to, and leverage their networks. The challenge is getting them to accept your invitation, and the best way to do that is to **personalize**.

Before I show you how to personalize your invitations and dramatically increase your chances for a positive response, I want you to take advantage of a powerful LinkedIn tool that allows you to reach out to strangers in a much more personal way: **LinkedIn Groups**.

> **Power play:**
>
> Send out 20-50 invitations every day to key influencers and decision makers.

LINKEDIN IS A TEAM SPORT: THE VALUE OF GROUPS

JOIN:

The fastest way to connect with someone completely out of your network is to join a LinkedIn group to which they belong. Once you identify a shared interest, something you and that person have in common, it's much easier to start a conversation or propose a casual meeting.

LinkedIn has groups of all kinds--alumni groups, special interest groups, social groups, etc. Whether you're a rugby player, a quilter, a software engineer or a stamp collector, odds are somebody in your industry loves those things too.

As LinkedIn becomes the mainstream platform for professional networking, people are less inclined to connect with random individuals or speak with total strangers. It's simple: if I were a top executive with lots of important relationships, I wouldn't make my profile available to everyone out there--I'd maintain a level of privacy to protect my contacts and my reputation.

Joining groups is the perfect way to bridge the gap: it not only helps you reach out to big names in your field, it allows you to connect with a wide range of people who may be able to help you. I highly suggest joining the group for your alma mater(s), along with those that relate to your personal interests (for example, hockey players, orchid growers, Dog Walkers of America). And, of course, the ones that revolve around your profession.

Once you join a group, you have immediate access to the profiles of its members, and the ability to connect with them directly. This doesn't mean you can (or should) join a group just because person A or B has it listed in their profile. In my experience, if you dig deep enough, you can find a common interest with nearly anybody you want to connect with, whether it's school, sports, hobbies, causes, etc.

Some groups don't accept everyone. To join them, you may need to prove you're on a certain career path, work in a certain industry, or know someone who's already a member.

> **Power play:**
>
> Join groups that will put you in touch with people who can help you land your next job.

These criteria help weed out folks looking to abuse the LinkedIn system. But, of course, that won't be you.

Connect:

LinkedIn groups give you an entry point for strategic networking, but it's up to you to make individual connections. Make sure to reach out to at least a few members as soon as you join a new group, then reach out to more each time you log on to LinkedIn.

You want to build a presence within each of these communities, so set aside a chunk of time every week (every day if your search is in high gear) to take advantage of the incredible power in numbers. Let me clarify: this is not about the power of numbers as in sending out hundreds of resumes. I hope by now we've put that misguided strategy to rest! I'm talking about the power of consistent, strategic activity, enhanced by the extraordinary potential of a network.

Make it personal

Whether you're reaching out to an individual or a member of one of your groups, you need to give the person a reason to accept your invitation.

The best opening play establishes a bond between you and the person you hope to engage. Did you go to the same school? Grow up in the same town? Do you share an interest, a hobby or belief in a cause? Are they connected to someone you know? Highlight these similarities to establish a connection more quickly and efficiently.

If you're a well-known athlete (amateur or professional), can you leverage your celebrity status to connect with fans?

Once you find something you have in common, mention it immediately in a personalized invitation:

Hello Kim,

As a fellow Colgate graduate and advertising executive, I'd love to connect with you here on LinkedIn. I'd also very much like to ask your

advice. Could we set up a call at your convenience? What works best for you over the next couple of days? Hope all is great.
Cheers,
Mark

I know what you're thinking: "Why send a personalized invitation with all that customized language when I can simply send the generic LinkedIn invite?"

Here's why: If you send me a generic invitation on LinkedIn, I'll almost always delete you. I won't give you a moment's thought because that generic text tells me you spent zero seconds thinking about who I am and why we should connect. If I see that you've written to me *because* of what I do, where I work or something I've expressed an interest in, I'm much more likely to be curious about you and consider your invitation.

This is crucial to the success of your online networking. **Personalize every invitation you send.** I always answer a personalized invitation, and the stats show that other LinkedIn users do, too. Studies reveal that over 60% of people accept invitations when they're personalized.

CUT, PASTE AND REPEAT

On my desktop, I have a Word document titled "LinkedIn templates" with a list of the personalized invites I like to use, whether they apply to a fellow Colgate University graduate, a member of a rugby player's group or financial regulatory association, or someone who shares another of my affiliations or interests. All I need to do is cut and paste the appropriate text into the invitation section, which allows me to invite multiple professionals in a very short time.

Let's say State Farm is on your list of 50 companies (and 200 jobs). You can run a LinkedIn search to pull up

> **Power play:**
>
> Use templates to send multiple LinkedIn invitations in a very short time.
>
> Just copy, paste and repeat!

everybody at State Farm who has basketball in their background, whether they played in college, professionally or as a weekend warrior. Then send them a personalized invite that highlights that common interest.

Hello Jorge,
As a fellow public speaker and basketball enthusiast, I thought it would be great to reach out and connect with you on LinkedIn. I'd like to set up a call in the coming days to ask for your advice and insight. Let me know what works best on your end. Hope all is great.
Best,
Mark

LinkedIn restricts the number of characters you can use in a personalized invitation. Currently, you're allowed 300. Make the most of the opportunity and try to use every one of those characters, but keep your templates within the limit so you can quickly paste your text and move on to the next invite. Just don't forget to change the name of the person you're writing to each time! To avoid this kind of error, I always triple check before hitting send.

Here's another example:

Hi Brad,
I see that you're a fellow Colgate graduate (marathoner, Yankees fan, gamer...) and that you work in the hospitality space. I'd love to connect here on LinkedIn and find out what it's like to work for Marriott.
Let's set up a chat in the coming days.
Regards,
Mark

Now you're thinking: "But what if this guy doesn't accept my invitation?"

Repeat after me: Who cares?

> **Coach says:**
>
> LinkedIn restricts the number of characters you can use in a personalized invitation.
>
> **LinkedIn limit: 300 characters**
>
> Watch for changes to their policy and be sure to keep your invites within those limits.

There's no limit on how many invitations you can send.

It often goes something like this: You send 100 (personalized!) invitations; 20 people accept right away and another 20 accept that night or the next morning when they check their emails; 20 more might respond a day or two later, and another 20 in a couple of weeks; 20 will delete or ignore your message.

Even if you sent 100 invites and only 20 people accepted, you'd still have 20 new connections with people who can directly impact your job search.

Do not agonize over every invitation. There are millions of people to connect with on LinkedIn. If you blow it with one or two or 10 of them...if you don't hear back from 100, it doesn't matter. All you need is to connect with one person who will lead you to your next great job, so please don't wring your hands--don't worry about every single word.

> **Coach says:**
>
> Do not agonize over each invitation you send!
>
> This is a numbers game: keep reaching out and your network will grow.

INCREASE YOUR CHANCES FOR A POSITIVE RESPONSE

As you've seen in this chapter, with consistent effort and a set of templates, you can send 100, or even 200+ invitations with minimal effort. At the same time, you can make it more likely that the people you reach out to will agree to connect.

A STRONG PROFILE

When a person receives your invitation, they'll often look at your profile before they decide how they want to respond. That's why your profile needs to look great. You've already taken care of that and you'll continue to fine-tune it as you learn more about industries and companies on your target list.

A PERSONAL TOUCH

> **Power play:**
>
> People shy away from requests for help but they love to share their expertise.
>
> Don't ask for help, ask for advice!

If you send personalized messages, each recipient will think, "Hey, there's a message here just for me!" They'll be flattered to know you took the time to compose a note for them. *You'll* be the one who gets the acceptance, not the person who sent the generic invite.

THE RIGHT "ASK"

Suppose you send an invite with this message: "Hi Katarina, I'd love to get your help. I'm looking for a job. Can I send you my resume?" How many people will be eager to accept that invitation? Very few. People are busy. They get requests all the time from within their existing network. Why would they welcome a stranger who's immediately making demands on their time?

If you ask for help right away, your response rate will stay very low. Instead, send an invite like this:

> *Hello Katarina, I'd love to get your advice. I'm considering a transition and I see you're at Colgate Palmolive. Would be great to know your thoughts on what makes a strong brand manager. I'd love to connect here and have a chat in the coming days. What works best on your end?*
> *Regards,*
> *Mark*

That's the high percentage invitation!

Manage your LinkedIn connections

Important reminder: As you add connections, it's essential to continue to look back on those connections you've already made.

In my opinion, the most effective way to manage your networking is with a spreadsheet of your connections. You can create an Excel spreadsheet on LinkedIn.

Download the spreadsheet and print out two copies, one sorted by your connections' last name and the other by the name of their company. You need both lists because if you want to get in touch with Bob Smith, you can find him quickly on a list sorted by last name. Then you can immediately grab his contact info and reach out to him. If you remember only that you have a friend named Bob at Coca Cola Co., you can find him listed under Coca Cola and you'll see that his last name is Smith. I use a printed list so I can highlight and make notes on connections I want to ask for a recommendation or follow up with by phone or by email.

As of the writing of this book, here are the steps you need to take:

- On your LinkedIn homepage, across the top menu, click on "My Network."
- Directly underneath "Your Connections," you'll see "See all." Click on "See all."
- You'll now see all your connections. Towards the upper right, click on the link that says, "Manage synced and imported contacts."
- On that same screen, towards the middle right, you'll see: "Advanced Actions." Underneath Advanced Actions, you'll see "Import Contacts." Click on "Import Contacts."
- You'll be prompted to choose your preferred format, either "fast file only" or "fast file plus other data." I recommend you choose "fast file only." Then click on "request archive."
- You'll receive an email from LinkedIn (approximately ten minutes later) with the option to Open the spreadsheet. Open it!

- Once you open the spreadsheet, you'll see six columns: First Name, Last Name, Email Address, Company Name, Position, Date Connected.
- You can now sort the spreadsheet by any of these columns. I suggest you create two versions of your list--one sorted by Last Name and the other by Company.
- To read the data, you'll need to expand the width of most columns.
- Highlight the entire file and sort by Column B (Last Name). You now have a list of all your connections sorted by last name. At this point, save this document, ideally on your desktop, and label it "LinkedIn Connections – Last Name – [Today's date]."
- Go back and sort again by Column D (Company Name) and save again, as "LinkedIn Connections – Company Name – [Today's date]."
- Some of you may choose to print these (I recommend this), allowing you to highlight and make notes. Others may choose to keep this on-screen and insert notes into the document itself. If you choose to print, be aware that if you want to follow my advice to print the first five columns, you'll need to adjust your right, left, top and bottom margins to the lowest settings so you can fit as much as possible on each page.
- Don't hit print until you scan through the document to be sure you're not printing multiples pages of column F, which you don't need.

You now have an easy-to-reference list of your connections. You can add notes or highlight high-priority people. This is a critical tool for your job search arsenal!

REACH OUT TO RECRUITERS – THEY STILL MATTER

As you continue your search, you'll come across or be contacted by re-cruiters. A good recruiter can be a huge asset in your efforts to land that ideal job, and the best advice I can offer to you when dealing with a re-cruiter is: *make a strong first impression.*

This is especially true if you're meeting with an executive recruiter. An often-ignored fact is that a company using an outside search firm is paying that recruiter a fee and the means to the fee is the candidate, which in this case means you! In attempting to fill a position, the recruiter will usually present only his or her best few candidates, so to make sure you're one of them, impress the recruiter right out of the gate.

I can safely say that in my 20+ years as a recruiter, most of my placements were candidates who lacked at least 30% of the "required" qualifications. So how did they get hired? Their lack of qualifications was overshadowed by their personality and the chemistry they had with the hiring man-ager and other members of the team.

> **Power play:**
>
> A good recruiter can be a major asset in your job search.
>
> Be sure to make a great first impression!

I've met with a couple thousand candidates and, trust me, as easygo-ing as I might seem in those meetings, I watch every move made and take in every word spoken. Not only do I want to earn the fee by making the placement, when I submit a candidate, my reputation is on the line.

To make a positive first impression on the recruiter: smile, have plenty of questions ready and present yourself as bright, articulate, ambi-tious, friendly and capable of adapting to most scenarios in a professional environment.

I believe that experienced executive recruiters at the top of their fields consider themselves your career agent, if you're a particularly impressive candidate. They'll represent you and push for you. They'll provide you with interviewing strategies and techniques, as well as substantial back-ground information about the company, group and individuals who'll interview you. And they'll offer you a variety of advice that will put you ahead of your competition.

This is why I consider meeting my candidates absolutely essential when I'm deciding which ones to represent, and why you should push hard to get a face-to-face meeting with the recruiter (assuming it's geographically feasible). Not only do you want to "put a face to your name," you also need to prove you can perform in an interview process.

Although it pains me to say this, a large percentage of recruiters throw resumes at the wall, hoping one will stick. So when you come across a recruiter who can align your interests with those of his or her clients, push for a meeting. Once you've made a good impression, it will be easier for that recruiter to represent you accurately and with greater enthusiasm. Make your first meeting memorable!

CHAPTER 8

TURN CONTACTS INTO CONNECTIONS

"Today I will do what others won't, so tomorrow
I can achieve what others can't."

~ JERRY RICE, NFL HALL OF FAMER

YOU'VE BEEN SENDING OUT A regular stream of invitations--personalized and targeted--to people who might be able to help you. You get an email that says, "Congratulations. You're now connected to Corey Miller." What do you do?

FOLLOW UP, FOLLOW UP, FOLLOW UP!

When you're notified that Corey has accepted your invitation, LinkedIn's confirmation email gives you the option to either look at his profile or move on. **Look at his profile.**

Why?

Because Corey has probably already forgotten you exist. As soon as he accepted your invitation, he got an email saying, "Congrats. You're now connected to (fill in your name)." And then LinkedIn whisked him away from your profile to a different page that says, "Other people you should know." You're now off his radar, a distant memory. But that's not a problem because you're about to follow up!

As soon as you get the email notification that Corey has agreed to connect, immediately click on "View Profile." On the right side of his profile, you'll see a tab for his contact information and a drop down that will provide his email address. Copy that email address, go out of LinkedIn and write directly to Corey via email.

In the subject heading, say: "Thanks for connecting."

In the body, write:

Hello Corey,

Thanks so much for accepting my invitation to connect on LinkedIn.

As I mentioned, I'm a fellow Colgate graduate and a hockey player, and I'd love to get your insight into what it's like to work at Turner Broadcasting. Also happy to catch up on all that is Colgate and hockey. Let's set up a chat in the coming days. What works best for you, Tuesday afternoon or Thursday morning?

You may notice I specified Tuesday afternoon and Thursday morning. That's called the "Alternate Sales Close": you always give people two options and ask them which one is better. It's an old sales technique I learned a long time ago and it works! If you just say, "I'd love to schedule a call in the coming weeks," they'll think, "Yeah, whatever. Talk to me in a couple of weeks." Then they'll definitely back-burner you and your request. You've got to put the onus on them to make a choice. They'll pick either Tuesday morning or Thursday afternoon because one of those days will be better than the other, and you'll be able to set up your call. If they come back saying neither works, suggest two other dates and times, again asking which is better.

Make sure to agree on the date and time, and follow up with: "If it's okay with you, I'll send you a calendar invite to make sure it appears on our schedules." Don't rely on anyone to put it into their own calendar. They may say they will, but it could slip their mind and when Tuesday afternoon comes around, they'll have completely forgotten about your call and booked something else during that slot.

Conversely, if someone reaches out to you and you think they would be a welcome addition to your network, accept their invitation right away and send a reply to thank them. **Make sure to reply via email and not within LinkedIn**, as most people do not keep their LinkedIn page open all day but check email frequently.

Take the next step and suggest a phone call because, after all, they thought highly enough of you to invite you into their network. This does not mean you should set up calls with everyone who invites you to connect. Pick those who may have direct access to key influencers and decision-makers.

REQUEST A PHONE CALL

Notice how in these initial, personalized exchanges, you always ask for a phone call. That's because a phone call is the perfect way to establish and grow professional relationships. When you're on the phone, you can talk to the person in a business-casual way, and have a relaxed conversation in which you can ask questions, request advice and be more like yourself. A phone call results in much more of an information-sharing experience.

As you speak with your new connection, make sure to engage her as soon as possible by discussing her career, company, position or the specifics behind your common connections and bonds. Ask how she got her start with the company or in her industry. Ask what developments she sees emerging within her field, and what sort of changes she might implement to improve performance at the company or within her group. Although it may seem like you're interviewing her, you're actually building rapport and establishing that you're the type of person she'd like to work with, someone who values her thoughts and opinions, as opposed to other candidates or colleagues who simply force-feed her their own ideas.

Once you sense that you've established that rapport, and you've injected a few comments that reinforce your potential in her industry, take the next step and ask for a meeting. You might say, "I see that you're also in New York City [or Chicago or Atlanta]. I'm going to be in your area for a couple of days next week, Tuesday afternoon and Thursday morning [again, the Alternate Sales Close]. Maybe we can grab a quick cup at Starbucks and pick up where we left off. I'd love your advice and insight on a potential transition I'm considering."

She's likely to accept because you're asking for advice, and many people are more than happy to show off their expertise and how much they know about their industry or company. Do you see how different this is from shoving a resume at them or hitting them up for a job? I'll talk more about what to do and say in these meetings in a future chapter, but I can't stress enough that it's essential to go after the phone calls, which lead to informal meetings, then interviews and offers!

How much is too much?

You'll be amazed at how many people respond well to your requests, but if you haven't heard back within a week, is it over? I say try again with something like,

> *Hi Stan,*
>   *I'm sure you're just as busy as I am, if not more, and my first note slipped between the cracks. (Insert here the body of your first email.)*

I've had many clients tell me they're uncomfortable reaching out a second time. They're afraid to seem like a pest and they don't want to overdo it, so they wait. I don't agree with that strategy. No one is going to get annoyed with you if you send them an email requesting a follow-up call once a week or every other week. Keep reminding yourself that you're pursuing your ideal job and building your future. Be tenacious! Imagine you're preparing for your next match, game, or meet. Push through any negative thoughts and focus on getting to your goal, which in this case is to lock down the call that will lead to the meetings.

MAKE IT WORTH THEIR TIME

We've already talked about making sure you put yourself in the place of the person you want to impress. What's in it for them?

That's why I keep reminding you not to ask for help, not to say you need a job, and definitely *not* to send your resume! You never ask, "Are you guys hiring?" or "Can I send you my resume?" Instead, you begin a dialog and let it develop from there. Any discussion of job opportunities should come from them, not from you. When they ask, "Are you looking now?"-- you can pause, ponder and calmly say, "Well, I'm considering my options..." Then they'll connect the dots and tell you if they're hiring.

When you call or email or chase somebody down, it's important to hold up your end of the exchange. You're not just asking, asking, asking. If you're a recently retired athlete, just out of school or new to a profession, you're probably wondering: what do I have to offer in return? More than you think! You'll obviously show them your appreciation and offer thanks for the advice you're getting, but on top of that, you might say, "Listen, if there's anybody in my network that can help you out in any way, please don't hesitate to ask."

Nobody does that right now. They don't say, "Hey, I know lots of people who might be useful for you to connect with--let's see what we can do for each other." Instead, they project something like: "I'm just a recent grad. What do I know? But can you help me? I really need your help! And here's my resume." By now you must see why that's not very effective.

> **Power play:**
>
> When you network, never expressly state that you're looking for a job.
>
> If they think it was *their* idea, they're much more likely to pursue you as a candidate.
>
> Let them connect the dots!

Show them the money

Another great tactic is to hint at the possibility of a bonus for them if you get hired. I'm not talking about a bribe here! Most large companies have an employee referral bonus program, which means that if your contact refers you and you get hired, he or she may receive an unexpected windfall, an extra $1000, $2000 or whatever the company provides.

Using Wells Fargo again as an example, if you've gotten to know someone there, even a little, you can reach out to them and say, "I see that you guys are looking to hire a trade support specialist and I was wondering if Wells Fargo has an employee referral bonus program?" Now your contact is thinking, "Ka-ching! This guy could be worth a couple thousand dollars to me... he seems pretty sharp...maybe I can help him get hired." You need to bring this up because even though employees have been informed, it's generally not foremost in their minds. Now you're more than just a potentially valuable addition to the firm. They've got a financial incentive to walk you through the hiring process internally.

No time like the present

One of the biggest keys to success in both job seeking and career development is persistence: regular, strategic action without long delays or drawn-out breaks. It can seem easy at times to get discouraged or put your search on hold--don't do it!

You've heard this phrase before, but it's worth repeating: **When you're on the hunt for a job, you can't turn off the momentum,** whether it's summertime, the holidays or vacations you've planned for yourself.

Even if people tell you (watch out for that bad advice!) that hiring managers are out of town for the summer, or that nobody's focused on hiring because it's the slow season...you've got to remain diligent. **Now is the best time, all the time.**

What if I told you that summer and holiday seasons are the perfect time to strike? When schedules free up a bit during the day, chances are the people you'd like to add to your network are finding more time in their schedule to connect. Send them an email or pick up the phone and call. When the weather heats up, invite them for a chat and an iced coffee. Show them that you're not letting the vacation vibes decrease your motivation to learn about what they do.

Something else to take advantage of: the competition for your ideal job is probably shutting down their efforts early to head for the pool. In other words, your chances of grabbing attention are HIGH. By the time the competition's tan begins to fade, you'll have forged new relationships and put yourself at the top of the hiring list. Then, when hiring managers find themselves under pressure to fill a spot, they'll think of you. And you'll be happy to remind them how impressed they were with you during the slow, summer months when everyone else was off the grid.

THAW OUT A HIRING FREEZE

That same logic applies to a hiring freeze. Over two decades, I heard hundreds of times from hiring managers and human resources professionals that their companies were in the midst of a hiring freeze and they didn't need my executive search services. It's an effective tactic to reduce the phone calls they get from recruiters, as well as the number of resumes they receive. This doesn't mean they're misleading us--their companies may truly have a freeze in place.

However, this almost always refers to their ability to hire new employees as additions to staff, not necessarily to replace employees who've left the firm. Therefore, a hiring freeze offers a unique opportunity to secure a position in that firm. The competition has already been scared away! If you connect with a hiring manager when a hiring freeze is on, ask if they're authorized to replace employees who've left voluntarily to go elsewhere. If the answer is yes, then nurture that relationship so you'll be the first person in line for the replacement position.

Keep your eye on the ball

The days of submitting your resume to an online portal and getting a call back are pretty much over. It's hard to believe, but all the time, energy and effort you spend filling out endless applications on company career pages or answering questions about "your greatest career achievements" rarely lead to interviews. It will only discourage you and take you off the path toward other, achievable opportunities. You know that already, but experience has taught me that I need to check with you again.

You're not doing that anymore, are you? If so, you've got to stop!

I take a hard stance on this topic because I'm absolutely convinced that the single most effective way to initiate meetings with people who can get you interviews is to make a professional connection with them on LinkedIn. It's really that simple.

Here's a quick recap of the plan to start leveraging your relationships on LinkedIn.

1) **Set your goals and stick to them**: Decide what kind of job you want, where you'd like to work and who can help you get there. Your target list must be strategic.

2) **Close in on your target(s)**: Once you've identified key influencers in your target areas, start connecting with them, but not all at once or too quickly. Take the time to personalize your invitations and follow up on every one. You need to show people you're genuinely interested in them.

3) **Leverage your acceptances:** When someone accepts your invitation but ignores the personalized message you included with it, don't leave things there. Most of the time, people don't respond, even with the email alert sent by LinkedIn. Using the contact information listed on their page, send a direct email to get things going. Make sure to repeat much of what you said in that personalized invite and give them compelling reasons to reply. Remember that networking is always a two-way street.

4) **Return the favor**: Use your first interactions (via email, phone or a casual meeting) to establish a productive exchange where you:
   * give your new contact a sense of who you are and what you can offer.
   * ask for their advice on how to break into or move forward in their field.
   * look for ways to help them in return.
5) **Don't give up or let up:**

Once you get started, keep working this plan. Leads will appear and, sooner than later, you'll be moving into the interviewing phase. Network your way into the job you want, one lead at a time!

CHAPTER 9

FIVE STEPS TO NETWORK LIKE A CHAMP

"There may be people that have more talent than you, but there's no excuse for anyone to work harder than you do."

~ DEREK JETER, MLB, 5X WORLD SERIES CHAMPION

THERE'S A RIGHT AND A wrong way to network. That may seem intimidating, but it's really a matter of applying a few simple principles that apply online, by phone or in person.

I've broken them down into five common-sense steps. As you put them into practice, they'll become almost second-nature to you.

1. **PREPARE**
2. **LISTEN**
3. **ENGAGE**
4. **OFFER**
5. **ASK**

DON'T BE SCARED, BE PREPARED

Whenever you arrange to speak with someone, whether they're a new contact from LinkedIn, someone you've run into at a networking event, or a referral from a friend, put yourself in their shoes. What will they get out of spending time with you? Why should they help you or offer advice? Give them a reason (give them several!), and consider the situation from their perspective.

Your starting point is always: **What's in it for them?**

Do your homework. Never enter a conversation without at least a general understanding of the industry, company and position you'll be discussing, as well as background information about the person you'll be speaking to. Have questions ready and practice answers to those you'll most likely be asked. The more you know, the better impression you'll make.

Don't expect anyone to educate you on things you can find out for yourself. It's not respectful of their time and it doesn't present you in a positive light. Show initiative. Demonstrate that you're capable of doing research and generating insights. If it's in the public domain, know about it before you engage. You never want a networking contact to roll her eyes and say, "Just Google it!"

Even better, prepare for future conversations before they've been scheduled. That way you'll never be caught off guard. If you're lucky enough to bump into someone who can help you, you'll have relevant questions (and answers) in your back pocket and you'll always be ready to impress!

You've got two ears but only one mouth – make sure you're listening!

One of the best skills you can develop is the ability to listen. Do you know the saying about how we've got two ears but only one mouth? It's especially relevant for networking.

Let's say you're at a barbecue and you run into somebody who could be a great connection for your job search, for example a V.P. of Finance. She's relaxed and happy to spend some time chatting. Do you barrage her with a list of your accomplishments or the services you could provide for her company? Do you ask an intelligent business question but then find you're not taking in her answer because you're frantically preparing your next insightful remark? Or maybe you open a discussion about a hot, industry trend, only to realize you have nothing to contribute on the topic...

How do you avoid these unwelcome scenarios?

If you've completed your step-one preparation, the best thing to do next is simply listen. Rather than stuff the conversation with your random or memorized thoughts, pay attention to what you're being told and ask questions that arise naturally from the discussion. Then make sure you listen carefully to the answers!

People love to share their thoughts on subjects related to their work or even to brainstorm ideas: these are both great starting points for a conversation. You don't want to seem like you're sucking up or sniffing around for insider information, you want to show that you're genuinely interested in these topics and in the viewpoint of the person you're speaking to.

Take the example of that V.P. of Finance at the barbecue. You might ask: "What are your thoughts on the Feds not changing the interest rates in the past few years as it relates to our industry? Do you see it changing in the future? What kind of hedge would you put in place to combat potential downturns resulting from that approach?" But don't fire away without taking time to hear her response. Follow the logical progression of ideas and let the discussion develop in a natural way.

Since you've done your prep work, you'll have a short list of questions in mind that sound conversational and fluid, even somewhat off-the-cuff. If you work these in based on what you're hearing and learning from your conversation partners, you'll be much more likely to impress them, as well as anybody listening in, thereby increasing your chances of generating interest in you as a possible hire.

If the person you're speaking to doesn't seem interested in giving their opinion, you can jump in with your own and say, "At my previous company, I was able to implement some of my ideas on helping team members work better together." Then add, always in a casual manner, "How do team members typically interact in your company?"

Make sure you spend less time speaking and more time listening, either to their opinion or their reaction to yours.

Stay attentive and mine these conversations for nuggets of job-seeking gold.

Focus not only on what a person says but how he says it. Don't rush to get your two cents in, or let your mind wander; you could miss a crucial piece of information or advice that might form the basis of future conversations. See if you can capture an esoteric point or two--it will enable you to remember the person much better and impress him with what you recall. Knowing what sports she likes or what music he listens to can give you a good talking point to lead with when you follow up.

Let the person talk and feel important. He'll look back on that conversation and remember how much he enjoyed it!

THE SECRET TO ENGAGEMENT: BUILD YOUR STORY AROUND THEIRS

You're becoming a pro at listening and asking questions--two skills that create a solid foundation for engagement. The following tips will help make your conversations more fruitful.

NEVER ask for help, ALWAYS ask for advice: People are much less inclined to engage when they think you're asking them for a job. In fact, they may use that opportunity to head for the bathroom, call home or get another drink. But most people love to talk about themselves and their careers and to see themselves as a valuable resource. In other words, they're happy to offer advice.

> **Coach says:**
>
> When you ask questions and get people engaged, they like you a lot more than when you do all the talking.

Show them you place a premium on their opinion and you'll often open the door to enjoyable, productive dialogue that can lead to interviews and even a hire!

Be ready with your answer to, "*What do you do?*" As we've seen, this question can make or break the conversation. If you don't know how to answer it, you may not get a second chance. Have a 20-second maximum reply prepared, with 2-3 sentences that describe your professional strengths and what you'll bring to your next employer.

Stay positive. Negativity can make people uncomfortable and put them on the defensive, especially in a social environment. It's one thing if they're put on the spot in a conference room during work hours--it's totally another at a cocktail party. Look (and talk) on the bright side to create and reinforce a positive impression.

Don't sell yourself, allow yourself to be bought! I'm always running across people who've been told, "Make sure you sell yourself!" Whether you're preparing for an interview, a networking event or any conversation that includes the question *What do you do?*...this is terrible advice.

In professional situations where we hope to impress, many of us tend to spew out a list of our accomplishments: *I've done X; I've done Y; this is what I'm great at!* Meanwhile, the people we're talking to stand there, eyes glazing over, nodding their heads and saying, "Wow, that's fascinating," while looking over our shoulder at the Yankees game on TV or wondering what's for dinner. They've lost us and we've lost them.

Quick exercise: Try to daydream or let your mind wander while you're talking to somebody, either in person or on the phone. I know you can't do it! But when you're listening, you can think about anything in the world and just nod your head, right? It's amazing. People can multitask, but they can't multi-think.

When you're talking about yourself in the context of your career, don't give your listener an opening to daydream or space out. When you speak to people, even face-to-face, if they're not interested in the topic, they can get distracted and "yes" you to death. You don't realize it and you keep talking. There's a great danger in this--you're selling yourself instead of building a relationship.

If you feel tempted to 'sell yourself' to a networking contact, stop! Remember that what you need to do is allow yourself to be bought. Ask questions that will reveal what she's looking to buy. Then, feed her information that will lead her to conclude you could be just the candidate she's looking for, or the perfect addition to her group. As I've said before, you want this to feel like it's *her* idea, not yours.

Retired athletes can be especially vulnerable to this sort of thing-- they're used to fans giving them a lot of attention. They may need to tone down descriptions of their athletic accomplishments and focus on what they can offer to the person in front of them.

Resist any tendency to brag: Maybe you batted .300 in 2008, but a hiring manager probably won't care. Here's a different approach: "Back when I played for the Mets, I was doing a lot of charity work and that got me very comfortable delivering a message to a large audience." That's what a hiring manager wants to hear! He'll be impressed and think, "Wow. This guy could have told me all about his athletic success but instead he's showing me how his background relates to what my company does and what we might need."

Have you ever entered a clothing store and been ambushed by a salesperson asking you immediately what you want to buy? Clearly his focus is on making the sale and not necessarily finding out what you need. And then there are times when a salesperson comes over, welcomes you and simply says that when you're ready to look for a specific size, he'll be over there in the corner folding sweaters. Rather than trying to sell you something you don't need, this salesperson is allowing you to buy what you want. I know which approach I'd prefer!

Don't go on and on about the $36 you saved your company back in 1998 by purchasing a different coffee machine, or the project you ran in 2004 to upgrade the company system to a long-extinct version of Windows. Give them very short highlights, in one or two sentences, of a recent success that's directly relevant to what they do.

"Earlier this year I showed our legal team how to save numerous hours when dealing with Dodd-Frank compliance issues, and I wrote a corporate handbook for counsel to use as a template going forward."

What you're doing here is not only addressing a time-management black hole for that person or that company's legal team, you're also showing how you were able to create a useful product, which instantly demonstrates the value you add and makes you a potential candidate for their firm.

RETURN THE FAVOR

In exchange for the information and advice you receive, you always want to provide something in return. As we've seen already, you have more to offer than you think! Here are some examples of what you do and don't want to offer:

Gratitude. Show appreciation for people's time and effort.
Admiration. Let them see that you're impressed by their achievements and expertise.
Assistance. Every business professional knows this rule: give to receive. Even if you lack experience in an area your contact is curious about, suggest people in your network who may be able to help or would be worthwhile networking contacts.

I know we've been over this but it bears repetition. Do not offer your resume too soon (if ever!)--it's an easy out for a contact, who may then cross you off her to-do list and move on. If a new connection asks right away to see a resume, even if you have one with you, do not hand it over! Tell her you'll forward it later, but urge her to look at your LinkedIn profile, which showcases a more complete picture of what you're all about.

It's critical to push immediately for meetings and referrals. Leave the resume for later and lead with your best sales product, yourself!

If you don't ask, you won't receive

Every time you interact with a professional contact, you've got an opportunity to get referred to someone else who can help as much, if not more. But the person in front of you may not think about that--you need to be proactive. Always ask if anyone in his network might be good for you to meet, or if he can introduce you (especially if you're at a gathering) to a key-influencer or decision-maker in your industry.

Chances are he knows someone but if you don't ask, he may not offer. What's the worst thing he can do? He may say nobody comes to mind, and then contact you later when he gets an idea. Remind yourself that the downside is just not that bad...so ask!

You also want to ask about next steps so you can schedule a follow-up in whatever form makes the most sense. You should always have a "call to action" to keep your contacts from forgetting about you. Let them know you're serious and worth meeting with again. Agree on what's next and follow up to be sure it happens.

Smile!

Okay, this is not officially part of the process, and it's often overlooked, but it's extremely effective. Even if your conversation partner is boring you to tears, please stay engaged and smile. If a direct connection with him won't help you, a link to someone in his network will, so keep reaching out and keep smiling.

CHAPTER 10

INCREASE YOUR PRESENCE, GROW YOUR BRAND

*"If you were disciplined enough to fight for something in
the sports world, then you will be disciplined enough to be
successful in the business world. Once you have been a winner,
you believe you can be a winner in everything you do. And in
the world of business, it's the winners that stay in business."*

~ Louise Ritter, U.S. Olympic gold medalist in high jump

WE ALL KNOW THAT A product, no matter how awesome, does not fly off
the shelves unless potential customers become aware it exists. Companies
invest a fortune in advertising, marketing and PR to let people know
they've got something to sell. As a job-seeker or career changer, you're
in a similar position. Of course, you're a hot commodity. But does your
future employer know that?

Little-known fact: LinkedIn provides you with free advertising for yourself!

Once you know how, you can spread the word about yourself and your capabilities in a way that will bring you to the attention of the people you want to attract.

In this chapter, I'll show you a variety of actions you can take to **get noticed and make connections on LinkedIn by adding value**. Try some of them. Try all of them. Hardly anybody is taking advantage of these extraordinary opportunities to promote themselves. By being the person who does, you'll surely stand out in the crowd.

Perform like an MVP

You can provide useful information to people in the industry you're targeting by posting relevant articles or anecdotes, or sharing someone else's material (just remember to make the appropriate attributions). The key is to make sure your postings are substantive--you won't draw positive attention by offering fluff. Post information to your own network and to specific groups. This allows you to showcase your knowledge or field of interest, while adding value without asking for anything in return.

Present yourself as a resource by offering assistance. When you send invitations, express your willingness to help. Many people tend to minimize their own value when they think about connecting on LinkedIn (or elsewhere). They consider themselves the one in need and forget that they, too, have accomplished a lot.

Don't be so humble. You're both professionals, so make the offer. Say "Please don't hesitate to reach out if there's anything I can do or if there's anyone in my network you'd like to connect with. I'd be happy to help." You can never create too much goodwill. Just be sure you mean it!

FOLLOW:

I've mentioned the importance of connecting with key influencers, people in your targeted profession who are looked on as authorities and have already gained a high degree of trust and respect in their field. On LinkedIn, you can follow people without necessarily connecting with them. (Just click the "follow" button on their profile page.) By following them, you'll keep abreast of the industry and, in time, you may even pop up on their radar and hear from them directly.

SHARE:

A great way to bring yourself to the attention of people you want to get to know, and to alert key influencers to your existence, is to share content you find useful and relevant. Most people appreciate when others help them grow their brand and, if you repost or comment on their articles frequently, they may notice and shoot you a thank you! Then you have an even greater opportunity to connect.

PARTICIPATE:

Leaving a comment on someone's post is the perfect way to join the conversation. Obviously, you'll only do this when you've read carefully and have something worthwhile to contribute. By engaging with others who are consuming and reacting to material that interests you, you'll become part of a community full of potential influencers, connectors and colleagues.

If someone else adds value by contributing to a conversation, show that you appreciate the input. Reach out right away with an invitation and a personalized note: "Hey, Maria – I really enjoyed your comments on [Contributor or Key Influencer]'s article. I hadn't thought of that angle. Thanks for bringing it to our attention!"

Every time you make an appearance on LinkedIn, you've got the chance to present yourself as knowledgeable, curious or passionate about a subject. When you interact with connections, group members or anyone who weighs in on a topic, you've got another potential contact--someone you can invite and add to your network. Make sure to keep your comments positive and on point.

THROW THE FIRST PITCH: PUBLISH YOUR OWN CONTENT

Now that you're connecting, you're setting up phone conversations. These conversations can lead to casual meetings, which can land you interviews in offices and eventually the offer you want. Don't stop building your network!

Another great way to access the right people, and something hardly anybody is doing on LinkedIn, is to create your own content. You do that by writing a brief article that highlights your expertise.

A financial analyst, for example, can talk about developments in Europe and how they're affecting the way banks are doing business, or maybe how new regulatory requirements are impacting investment decisions.

If you want to get into real estate, you can research and write something like: *Four critical steps to take when buying a home.* Or maybe: *The four worst mistakes first-time home-buyers nearly always make.* Then write content around four critical steps to take (or avoid) when buying a home.

If you're transitioning from athletics to the business world, you can write something like *Six winning characteristics an athlete brings to the boardroom.* Keep it short, no more than 600 words, because you want to capture the reader's interest without giving away too much of your knowledge. Begin to build your authority and set yourself up as an expert, but always leave them wanting more.

Whatever your background, I promise, you can write three or four paragraphs that showcase your skill set, your capabilities and your knowledge. And your little article will put you in a completely different category from most job seekers who have no clue.

These articles do NOT need to be perfect. You're not aiming for a Pulitzer Prize. Just write a few paragraphs and post them in LinkedIn's Pulse section. Then get ready to see tons of people reading what you wrote.

WRITE AN ARTICLE--IT'S MUCH EASIER THAN YOU THINK!

Many people panic at the thought of writing an article. But it's so much easier than you think. Here's what you do:

Decide what you want to write about.
One article = one simple, relevant, engaging idea.

Imagine you're chatting with a friend or colleague about a topic related to your chosen profession. Use a casual, conversational tone. Think of this as talking, not writing.

Then follow these six steps and you'll be fine:

1. Describe your idea in a headline. The headline is your promise to the reader: it tells them exactly what they'll get from your piece.
2. Start with a couple of sentences to introduce what you'll talk about.
3. List three to five points that support the case you're making.
4. Write a short headline (a sub-head) for each of your three to five points.
5. Flesh out each of those points in one to two short paragraphs.
6. Wrap up with a recap and a conclusion.

That's all you need!

You could set yourself the goal of posting once a week. The more content you put in rotation, the more people you'll reach, and the more people will think, "Hey, I wonder who this guy is. Let me check him out." Someone may look at your profile and say, "Wow, we want to talk to this woman." Or: "We need to connect with this guy. That was a fabulous article about bringing athletic expertise to the workplace. We need someone like this at our company." Then you're off and running!

At the end of your piece, be sure to tell your readers what you want them to do next. In other words, include a "Call to Action."

It goes something like this: *"If you think this post delivered some great ideas, please share it with <u>three</u> of your connections and fellow group members, and post it on your other social media platforms. I've picked up great ideas this way from other thought leaders here on LinkedIn. And naturally, please leave your comments below. I really want to hear your thoughts on this topic!"*

Then take that article and share it with a bunch of the groups you belong to. Some of those groups may be small, but others might have 200,000 members. Imagine if 200,000 people had access to your story! With LinkedIn groups, they do. Some of them will notice your post, some will read it, and many may say, "This person knows a whole lot about

> **Power play:**
>
> The power of 3.
>
> Studies have shown that asking your readers to share your article with 3 people leads to a better result, not only because it's a specific call to action but because 3 has proven to be the most effective number.

currencies (or real estate or marketing or valuable traits athletes bring to the boardroom)...we need someone like this at our firm." That kind of reaction can apply to whatever you write about.

SHARE YOUR ORIGINAL CONTENT WITH YOUR GROUPS

When it comes to publishing your own content, the power of groups is incredible. This is where the math kicks in and can boost your results through the roof! Add your Call to Action at the bottom of the article, inviting people to comment, share and connect, and this is basically an invitation to advertise yourself and your brand.

Once you've written your article and posted it on LinkedIn (by clicking "Submit"), the piece will automatically be shared with your network.

To share with your groups, after your article has been published, click the "Share on LinkedIn" icon. You'll be asked for the title (make sure it's an attention-grabber!) and a short blurb to describe your piece (about 50 words that make absolutely clear what's to be gained from reading it). Then you'll have the opportunity to type in the names of the groups you want to share with.

When sharing with groups, you must enter the name of each group manually.

Here's what I do: I type each letter of the alphabet and see which groups pop up. Then I pick the ones that are appropriate and I move on to the next letter. Share with as many groups as you can – your goal is to maximize your exposure.

> **Coach says:**
>
> There are many excellent resources available on how to write attention-grabbing headlines.
>
> Here's my favorite:
>
> http://coschedule.com/headline-analyzer

Let's say you post your article for home-buyers to the Quilting Association of America group. A random quilter in that group may also happen to be (or know) the head of development for a top real estate firm in your city. That person, impressed with your knowledge of existing market conditions, may reach out and connect with you or refer you to somebody else with similar interests.

As your article spends time on LinkedIn and attracts more readers, people will like it, share it and leave comments. It's imperative to review their profiles and identify those you'd like to connect with. Then send each of them a personalized invitation.

Hello Mike,

I'm very glad you liked my recent article on buying a home. I'd love to connect with you here on LinkedIn and set up a call to formally introduce ourselves.

Regards,

Mark.

How easy is that?

Anyone who takes the time to leave a comment, share or even like your article demonstrates that they find your perspective appealing. These are people you may want to connect with. When someone leaves a comment, reply as soon as possible--while the topic remains fresh in people's minds.

If a comment is intended to create an argument or promote major disagreement, do not take the bait! Simply state that you respectfully disagree and defend your position again.

Most people leave very positive comments. In those cases, thank them and reinforce any point they reference from your article. You may also want to add that you'd be happy to discuss the issue in more detail by phone. What you're trying to do by writing content is create significant engagement between you and prospective hiring managers or key influencers. An original article that showcases your capabilities in a specific area or industry is effectively advertising your brand to a set of people that might include your next employer.

Here's how

Write, post and share your content.

1. Where it says, "Post an article," click on that yellow button. You'll be asked "What do you want to write about?"
2. Add your title. Make sure it captures the attention of your intended audience by solving a problem they struggle with or making a promise they can't resist.
3. Your picture will automatically pop up. If you like that one for this purpose, fine. You can also select another one and upload it.
4. Write your article. As I mapped out above, it's easier than you think!

5. At the end of your article, include a Call to Action.
6. Once you finalize the piece, check (or have someone else check) your spelling and grammar, then hit "Publish."
7. Now share! Not just with your network but with members of your groups.

GUEST POST ON SOMEONE ELSE'S BLOG

To expand your reach even further, consider guest posting on the blogs of people in your industry. Watch for (or seek out) opportunities to contribute to newsletters, blogs, online resources, magazines, etc. Just be sure you stay on brand. In other words, create content that demonstrates interests relevant to that next job you're hoping to land.

Whenever one of your articles gets published elsewhere, share it on LinkedIn with your network and your groups. This will widen your appeal and build your reputation.

I'm a *Forbes* contributor, and as soon as my *Forbes* articles appear, I make sure to share them with my LinkedIn network and groups. You may also want to share your content on your Facebook page, your Twitter feed and your other social media accounts.

Social media exposure most likely worked to your advantage during your athletic career. In the world of job searching and career building, your social media exposure can broadcast the experience you bring and make clear why you'd be a great hire.

Fourth Quarter
Ace Your Interviews and
Land Your Offers

CHAPTER 11

THE LINE-BUSTING ADVANTAGE OF INTERVIEWING WELL

"Obstacles don't have to stop you. If you run into a
wall, don't turn around and give up. Figure out how
to climb it, go through it, or work around it."

~ MICHAEL JORDAN, NBA HALL OF FAMER, OLYMPIAN

YOU'VE MADE IT TO THE quarterfinals!

You've gotten to the interview phase of your job search and have been invited in-house to meet with a potential employer or colleague.

Considering all you've done to get here, you might feel exhausted. After endless networking, speaking with recruiters, pitching yourself to friends and family members who may know of someone hiring, and filling out job applications, you might think your resume and connections should speak for themselves in the interview room. It's clear you're talented or you wouldn't be there, right?

This is a common mistake you need to avoid.

Remember that you still need to sell yourself…ok, I'm kidding, please don't do that! As I've explained regarding networking, you should **let yourself be bought!**

Don't rattle off your qualifications. Don't dive right in with a list of reasons why they should hire you.

Engage in a dialogue with your interviewer. In the course of that conversation, listen, ask relevant, insightful questions. Insert (pre-planned) details about your unique value as if they're coming to you spontaneously, and prove to the hiring manager you're the best person for the job.

A lot goes into making that happen. This chapter will set you up to walk in with confidence and walk away knowing you did everything you could to land an offer.

Interviewing is a two-way street

Many candidates get overly confident at this stage of the game. That mistake can mean the difference between getting a job or never hearing from that employer again.

Through thoughtful and careful preparation and practice, you'll not only improve your chances of making it to the next round of the interview, you'll also be in your best interview shape and fired up to meet with potential employers and colleagues at numerous places. Which means you're far more likely to have the option of choosing between multiple offers and accepting the job that suits you best.

Interviewing is a two-way street. You are considering them as much as they are considering you. An interview or series of interviews at a company you think you'd like to work for is an opportunity for both sides to ensure you're an optimal "fit."

While they're grilling you on your background and experience, you're also learning about the job and the company culture, and getting a chance to see if these are people you want to spend time with, day after day.

With each interview, you find out more about the kind of job you want and how to present yourself in the best light to get it.

If you're looking for a sparring partner, you want to get in the ring with him first. If you're looking for a tennis buddy, you want to hit with her before you commit to meeting every week. Same idea.

The interview is your chance to make something happen--if not this position today, maybe the one you'll be shooting for tomorrow.

Below are three no-brainers many people forget:

* Be on time! That means 10-15 minutes early.
* Bring a couple of copies of your resume. Now is the time to provide one, if requested.
* Show up ready to speak about what the company does and how you'll fit in as both new hire and long-term employee. This chapter will give you what you need to do that well.

Bring your A game

In my nearly thirty years of interviewing candidates and preparing them to meet with potential employers, I've identified six core strategies to help you ace your interviews, not only in the next round of your current job search but for the rest of your career.

You can think of them as a process but the order is not critical. What matters is that you keep all these steps in mind before you show up and while you're in the room.

Six techniques that set you up to bring your A game:

1. **Anticipate what they need.**
2. **Answer like you knew what they would ask.**
3. **Act positive: live by the PnP rule.**
4. **Ask the questions that will land you the job.**
5. **Always practice!**
6. **Attitude is everything.**

ANTICIPATE WHAT THEY NEED

I've said this many times but it's so important I need to keep repeating it:

Put yourself in the place of your interviewer and anticipate what he's looking for.

What skills, capabilities, and qualities does he need most from the person who takes this position?

How will he decide which of the ten candidates he's interviewing will be the best choice for the job?

We all know hiring managers don't necessarily choose the smartest person they interview (any more than the tallest, loudest or funniest). They hire the person they'll feel most comfortable sharing an office with 8-12 hours a day, someone they can rely on to get the job done and make them look good to senior management. Seriously. It's that simple.

LET'S NOT OVERTHINK WHY YOU'LL GET HIRED!

> **Power play:**
>
> Remember to always put yourself in the place of the people interviewing you. Anticipate their needs and what they're looking for.

So how do they choose that one person? It's a lot like those reality TV shows where the winner's the one who survives the obstacles and is still there at the end, after everyone else has been eliminated. And it's often *not* the person you expected when the show began! Think of it as an obstacle course--you just need to come through the process unscathed. In an interview or a round of interviews, that means making sure you avoid mistakes and don't say anything that raises objections or concerns.

What will it take to win?

As an athlete, you know how important it is to train. The more you run sprints, take jump-shots, practice your skating or step into the batting cage, the more you experience different scenarios and the more you can anticipate what might happen in an upcoming match. You try out new moves. You build muscle memory. You get better at what works and get rid of what doesn't.

Then, when it's game time, you're ready.

With interview preparation, your training ground looks a little different but it functions in a similar way. It's not a court, field or arena. It's (are you ready?)...a pad of paper. A lined legal pad. A spiral notebook. Maybe a few pieces of loose-leaf. This is where you'll work through likely interview scenarios and prepare in advance so you can triumph.

Studies have shown that the brain retains more information when content is written on paper rather than typed out or memorized. That's why you need to write these things down.

Get out your pen!

Make a list of the skills, industry knowledge, personality traits and anything else you would look for if you were the manager in charge of filling this role.

For a position in business development with a sporting goods manufacturer, the ideal candidate would have some background in sales, the confidence to speak directly with internal and external senior management, an ability to think on his feet, and a high level of comfort in pressure-filled situations.

A lawyer at a financial services firm would most likely need extensive knowledge of the relevant financial products, a solid understanding of the legal framework in the documents to be negotiated and drafted and, maybe most important, the right personality for dealing directly with the trading desk, outside counsel and senior management.

ANSWER LIKE YOU KNEW WHAT THEY WOULD ASK

Take a long look at the list you've just compiled. Remember, you're still acting as the hiring manager.

Now write down all the questions you would ask candidates based on what you feel the job requires.

Go beyond the usual, boring ones like: "What are your strengths and weaknesses?" or "Why should I hire you?" And don't choose easy, yes-or-no questions that telegraph the answer you're looking for.

If you want the (by now cliché) "team player," don't say: "So, Stan, are you a team player?" Ask for a specific example of a time when teamwork was needed, and how he pulled with his group to make something happen. In the business development example above, you could inquire about a deal the candidate developed--what it entailed, how he went about it and how it turned out.

Once you've listed the questions you believe the hiring manager will ask, **write down the answers you'd consider most effective.**

Keep these answers clear and to-the-point. Don't go on any long-winded journeys through the course of your life or your career. Nobody cares how your grandmother taught you the importance of a strong work ethic after she lived through the Great Depression. Interviewers want a concise, compelling response to the question they've asked.

Working through these questions and answers in the training space of your legal pad lets you craft grand slam responses in advance: responses that showcase your expertise, your experience and your personality, and prove to your listener you're the right one for the job.

TURN DEFENSE INTO OFFENSE

Most of the time a hiring manager will review your resume before she meets you to make notes of things she's either curious or concerned about. She might circle a few lines, put a question mark in red ink, or leave some other reminder to explore that issue.

Start by preparing for the overused and dreaded questions: "Where do you see yourself in five years?" and "What can you tell me about yourself?"

If your first instinct is to Google the top five responses…go for it. But you'll probably end up with something generic (which the hiring manager has heard many times), and you'll be left wondering if that got you anywhere. Instead…

Whenever you're asked, "where do you see yourself in five years?"-- toss the question back!

Reply with: "I have a few ideas about where I'd like to be in that time frame. However, I'd like to hear from you what opportunities might be available to someone in this position over the next five years." The hiring manager will probably respond with three or four directions you might take in that role, and at that point, based on what you've heard, you can choose the ones that seem appealing.

Another of my favorite interview scenarios (note the sarcasm, please) is a hiring manager who says: "Tell me about yourself." Do they really want to hear all about you? Not a chance in hell! Once you start working there, you can share lunch with your former interviewer and tell her who inspired you to take ceramics in high school. For the purposes of getting you hired, there's a much better way to answer the question.

As an applicant for a position, you've provided the company with an overview of your accomplishments through a resume, an application form or a conversation with someone in Human Resources. They may also have access to content you've created. They do not want to hear you repeat all this back.

> **Coach says:**
>
> I don't even like to address the "name your weakness" question. It's useless and doesn't come up as often as people think. It won't come up at all if you follow my advice about steering the interview into a conversation!

The interview is a place to build on what they already know by adding details or new information and, at the most, offering a quick recap of the basics. Start with something like, "As you can see, I have a fairly extensive background in media relations. Is there anything you'd like me to discuss in more detail?"

This is a great reply because it:

- saves them from hearing a whole lot of stuff they don't care about.
- takes them off the hook if they've forgotten (or neglected to review) anything essential.
- prompts them to ask you about something they have a specific interest in.

You'll soon learn how to avoid many of these standard scenarios by guiding the conversation, as you seed the interview with information you want people to know, anecdotes that show what makes you tick, and ready-to-go questions that prove how insightful and resourceful you are.

PUT YOURSELF ON THE ROPES

We all have some kind of elephant in the room: a situation or an issue in our background that we hope they won't ask about...and what happens? They always do!

Take out that yellow pad again and write down all the questions you would ask yourself if you were a hiring manager trying to put a candidate on the defensive. In this case, the candidate is you, so you know better than anyone where the weak spots lie.

Let's say Isiah has had four jobs over the past four years. Maybe he just happened to work for companies that went out of business, or he followed a partner to another firm, or simply made a move each time that seemed right for his career--all legitimate reasons. Isiah needs a convincing explanation for each of those transitions.

Gabriella may have left an MBA program just a few credits short of receiving her degree. You might conclude that she's a quitter, or she just couldn't hack it. It's also possible, though, that an urgent family situation caused her to leave school, or she ran out of funds for tuition.

From his resume, it looks like Michael retired earlier than necessary from a lucrative basketball career. You'll want to know why, and you'll need to be reassured that if you hire Michael, he won't leave your company at the top of his game.

Read carefully through your resume. Drill deep and find the issues that could throw you off balance. Then write out clear, concise responses and be ready to deliver them with confidence. Which brings us to the PnP rule...

Act positive: live by the PnP rule

When faced with a hard interview question, one that seems to address a weakness or a negative in your prior work experience, always take the PnP approach. Start with a positive statement (P), which highlights elements that will be viewed favorably. Then address--directly but briefly--the negative element (n), and end with another positive statement (P) to underscore how the potential negative was converted into big positive for you and your career.

Most people remember the first and last comments in a reply, but not so much the middle. And they'll be impressed by how you turned a deficit into victory.

If you were let go at your job, start like this: "It was an amazing opportunity to work at a great company with like-minded people, but when they consolidated the business

> **Here's how:**
>
> The PnP rule means always cushion a negative by placing it between two positives.
>
> 1. Start with a positive statement.
>
> 2. Slip in your negative.
>
> 3. Finish with another positive.

unit and had to let several team members go, it became a blessing in disguise. It gave me the time and resources to explore other areas of interest, and now I'll be able to leverage my experience there into a position like the one we're discussing today."

Stay positive: speak well of those you worked with (nobody wants to invite a complainer or a gossip into their midst), and demonstrate your ability to remain optimistic and thrive within a team structure, especially if it's clear that your morale took a hit.

ASK THE QUESTIONS THAT WILL LAND YOU THE JOB

The fourth step of your interview preparation is possibly the most important. It can determine how you'll be seen and where you'll rank among all candidates considered for the position.

How many times have you been in an interview where they asked, "Do you have any questions?" Almost everybody flounders here. They either draw a blank, reply that everything's already been covered, or ask questions that fit into what I call the "interview box." "Interview box" questions are the ones everyone tends to ask: what are the day-to-day responsibilities? the required skills and team structure? And where's the company cafeteria?

Ask questions outside that interview box!

What do I mean?

First things first--you need to get those questions ready. Before your interview, you'll research not only the company considering you, but also the people who work there. I recommend (no surprise here!) LinkedIn. If you can't find them there, run a search on the browser of your choice.

Take notes on work history, education, affiliations and groups. As always, look for those common bonds--something you share with each interviewer that could steer the conversation off the typical, formal path. You want that common interest or connection established as soon as possible, ideally within the first few minutes.

Never forget that the interview process is intended to filter people out (like that reality show where you want to stay on the island). Hiring managers are looking for the person they'll most enjoy working with, and who'll be able to accomplish the tasks at hand from day one and going forward.

They want to hire someone who'll work hard, get things right, be a positive influence on others, and make them look good, remember?

Okay. You want to ask great questions. But what are they?

Let's take a step back.

Think about the last time you were in a social setting (at a BBQ, in a bar, at the gym, etc.) and chatting with a friend about a sports team's performance. Let's say you were discussing the NY Yankees pitching staff.

My guess is that it went something like: "Mark, the Yanks need to get another starting pitcher, and fast. They're dropping out of the race and if they don't address that need, it's lights out." My reply might be, "Brett, you couldn't be more wrong. They need another outfielder; they can't keep losing these low-scoring games with such a low octane offense."

Notice how each of us began by blurting out our own opinions, without giving a thought to what the other had in mind?

Imagine starting the conversation a different way: "Brett, I know you pay a lot of attention to the Yankees. In your opinion, what do they need to do right away to improve their chances at the playoffs?" I promise you that Brett will be floored that you asked for his opinion first, instead of trumpeting your own. He'll be flattered and likely see you in a positive light.

Never let go of that core technique when it comes to both your network and your interviews: LISTEN!

LISTEN FIRST AND PEOPLE WILL BE FAR MORE INTERESTED IN WHAT YOU HAVE TO SAY

The ideal questions focus on the industry you're interviewing in, and the work being done outside the role you've applied for. Most important, they ask for the interviewer's opinion.

"Susan, I noticed on your website's news feed that your firm just signed a $20M deal to expand into the Nordic countries now that your new light-weight ski boot is gaining traction overseas. In your opinion, where else might be a growth opportunity for the product, and how do you think you could gain a foothold there?"

That question will push you to the front of the line!

Think about it: your question involves a positive news story about Susan's company, which demonstrates that you keep up with industry developments, and, best of all, you want to know what she has to say about the whole thing. Now she's thinking, "Here's a candidate who actually cares what I have to say! The others I met were so caught up in their own worlds, they barely paid attention to what I contribute to my firm."

There's a wide variety of questions you can ask. Always have at least three or four ready, and ask them as early as possible. This turns the interview into a conversation about the business rather than an investigation of your weaknesses!

One more time…

The sooner you turn the interview into a conversation about the business and both your roles in it, the more likely you'll be offered the job.

Warning! If you feel during the interview that the position is not right for you, if you're either over- or under-qualified, do NOT change your attitude, your momentum or your performance in any way. In my many years of recruiting, there have been numerous times when the interviewer told me afterwards that my candidate was not a fit for that specific job, but would be great in a different one. In other words, they were interested in extending an offer for a more appropriate position.

> **Coach says:**
>
> One of my favorite things to do when coaching clients is to help them come up with hole-in-one questions--shots that allow them to win the tournament and get the offer!

Remind yourself that you chose to put that company on your target list, so getting in the door there was your goal. If you stay on track and impress the hiring managers, they can find a way to bring you on board.

ALWAYS PRACTICE!

When you're trying out for a team or playing a sport, you need to practice intensely. The same applies to landing a job.

If you've followed the **WIN AGAIN** playbook so far, you've reviewed your background and experience to identify the skills and personality traits that make you attractive as a candidate. You've networked like a champ and landed at least one, if not more interviews. You're preparing for those interviews by drilling deep into your resume, your personal story (your brand), and figuring out what a hiring manager will want to ask about. You've written down (on paper!) a list of questions to expect and the answers you'll have ready.

Now take those notes to your kitchen, your bedroom or the park, or get on the phone with a friend and **practice your answers**. Repeat them over and over until you're clear about how you'll say them and what kind of energy you'll bring. Think about why you're eager for this opportunity and make sure that enthusiasm comes through when you speak. Let me be very clear:

IF YOU DON'T PRACTICE FOR YOUR INTERVIEW, YOUR CHANCES OF SUCCESS ARE SLIM!

If you do practice, though--especially if you follow the steps I've outlined for you here--you'll rise above your competition, you'll make a strong impression and you'll feel great, not only about yourself but about the interview experience.

Attitude is everything

An important word of encouragement: make sure you express your excitement about the company. Too many people miss this crucial part of getting a job. Don't leave it to your interviewer to figure this out: **Say you want to work there!** It's fine to let them know that you love the company, you've researched it thoroughly, you understand their culture and would love to be a part of it.

You can interview your pants off but forget this and ruin your chances. Hiring managers have often said to me, "Tom was great and we really liked him, but he didn't seem all that interested. He never actually said he wanted to work for us." Don't be that person. Prepare, practice and show your enthusiasm.

Smile as much as you can throughout the interview, ideally without looking insincere! It's often

> **Power play:**
>
> When you meet with a potential employer or colleague, make clear that after researching the company and meeting with some of the people, you're excited at the prospect of working there.
>
> Show your enthusiasm!

said that people have a much higher regard for someone who smiles as they respond. It will make you appear confident about your answers and demonstrate the positive mindset that hiring managers seek.

If you invest enough time in your interview preparation, you'll walk in with a "Bring it on!" attitude because you'll be ready for any question. When you're confident, congenial, inquisitive, and knowledgeable about the business and industry, you'll outpace your competition so you can lap the field and win the race to the offer.

CHAPTER 12

PUSH IT OVER THE GOAL LINE: INTERVIEW FOLLOW-UP

"It isn't the mountains ahead to climb that wear
you out; it's the pebble in your shoe."

~ MUHAMMAD ALI, WORLD HEAVYWEIGHT CHAMPION BOXER, "THE GREATEST"

TOO MANY PEOPLE PUT ALL their effort into the interview and then walk away without proper follow-up: an error that can mean the difference between a pleasant conversation and a meeting that leads to an offer!

BEFORE YOU LEAVE THE ROOM

You've made it through the interview, you're shaking hands with the interviewer(s) and you're about to say goodbye. Don't leave yet! You need to take care of a couple of things.

* Get contact information for the people you've just met. If they didn't hand you a business card before or during your meeting, ask for one. Or collect that information in any way that works for

you: write it down, put it in your phone, send yourself a text or an email.

* Find out who you should follow up with.
* Ask how long their decision process should take.

As you'll see below, it's essential to stay on their case, and you need to do that in a subtle, appropriate way.

On the way home

If you're walking a few blocks after your interview (to a subway, bus, taxi or your next destination), stop at a coffee shop, sit down, order something and take a deep breath. Then pull out your notepad and start writing (remember how important it is to do this by hand)! Make a few notes regarding your performance, what you think went well, what may have raised concerns, and any details you can reference in a future conversation.

Recapture, as best you can, how they answered the great questions you asked (the longer you wait to do this, the more difficult it will become). Jot down the fact that you discussed last night's Bulls game. Think about everything you saw and heard in their office space. List your observations about people working there and the overall "vibe." Not only will this information serve you well in later interviews, it will help you decide whether you want to join that company or choose another.

Later that day

Later that day or early the next morning (don't wait beyond that!), compose an email for each interviewer. Thank them for their time and, most importantly, remind them of two to three of your skills or personality traits that will be crucial for a successful hire. Add a follow-up to one of the questions you asked to keep the conversation moving forward. Your follow-up can be a new question, further thoughts on something you discussed, or a link to relevant information or a piece of content they're likely to find useful.

Here are those steps again. Write an email for each interviewer that will:

* thank them for their time
* point out a specific topic you discussed that you bring up again later
* remind them of two or three of your skills or personality traits that will make you successful in the position
* include some form of follow-up / call to action to keep the dialogue going

Hello Anna,

It was a pleasure meeting with you today.

I'm still amazed at how much of a small world we live in. I would have never guessed that my good friend Adam happens to be your literary agent, how about that!

After our meeting, I considered again the factors that I believe will allow me to hit the ground running with your team. I truly enjoy speaking in front of big crowds, and thus will be comfortable presenting in an investor relations capacity. I have years of experience being interviewed and speaking to the camera, and my career as an athlete memorizing a playbook allows me to climb any steep learning curve quickly.

I plan on calling Adam later to relate my connection to you, he'll be thrilled to hear we have met.

I look forward to continuing the process with your group.

Best Regards,

Mark

Naturally, I would be remiss if I didn't strongly urge you to send each interviewer a LinkedIn invitation (also sent by the following day), with a personalized message reading something like this:

> *Hello Anna,*
>
> *Thank you for sharing your time with me yesterday. Your insights into the position and your firm were extremely helpful, and I am very interested in becoming a member of your team. Let's connect here on LinkedIn, and please don't hesitate to reach out for any reason.*
> *All the best,*
> *Mark*

WHAT NEXT?

You've sent your follow-up emails and LinkedIn invites, and now you're waiting for the post-interview phone call or emails. If you

> **Here's how:**
>
> Follow up with each interviewer by email.
>
> 1. Thank them for sharing their time.
>
> 2. Remind them of what makes you an ideal candidate.
>
> 3. Keep the dialogue going.
>
> 4. Send invitations to connect on LinkedIn.

went through a recruiter, make sure to contact him right away with your feedback and tell him your level of interest in the position. You should also let him know how you would tackle any tasks you don't yet have experience with. Remember: you thought these through before the interviews and wrote your answers down! This will give the recruiter ammunition to discuss issues with the hiring manager and satisfy any concerns.

Now the waiting begins. A day goes by. A few more. It's been a week since you heard anything. You're wringing your hands, wondering when the heck you should follow up again. Why aren't they calling? You're a perfect candidate and you kicked butt in the interview. Or did you?

Maybe you goofed up an answer. You had an odd expression on your face when you shook their hands... or the questions you asked really weren't so great after all... Maybe you're too old. Maybe your competition is stronger. Maybe ... just stop!

After nearly 30 years of executive search experience, I can safely say that most hiring decisions stretch out over weeks or months, not days or hours, and that delays rarely have anything to do with the candidates. Decisions take longer than expected for any number of reasons, from hiring managers on vacation to new projects or developments that make it impossible to evaluate interviews right after they happen.

None of these reasons should prevent you from following up. But how do you do that without seeming like a pest and landing yourself on the scrap heap of rejected candidates?

The best way to follow up is not to follow up.

What?

Remember this pillar of the *WIN AGAIN* playbook:

Don't Sell Yourself – Allow Yourself to be Bought!

That means you will NOT send an email that screams, "I am following up on my interview." While that message reflects your interest, it also can also position you as desperate. Even if that's the case, they don't need to know it!

To keep things casual and confident, send a note referencing a point or two about the industry, made in the interview by either you or your interviewer. Or refer to one of the questions you asked, adding some detail, providing additional information or requesting an opinion. Send that note no more than two days after your interview. That should compel her to respond, especially if you don't reference your interview or the open position.

If she doesn't reply, send another note two days later, with a direct mention of something about her--something she said, or any professional activity she's involved in.

You'll see a much higher rate of engagement with hiring managers once you reference them and their work, and they'll rate you that much higher because of your post-interview dialogue (that isn't a follow-up!).

IF YOU DON'T GET THE JOB

One last point for this chapter: if you find out you won't be receiving an offer, it's essential to send a follow-up note stating that you remain very interested in the company and any future openings that may emerge, and that you'd like to keep in touch. Give your interviewer a compelling reason to stay connected by letting her know you'll be happy to introduce her to anyone in your LinkedIn network who might be helpful to her career. Stay relevant, be helpful, and keep cool (even if you don't feel that way!).

Ignore that last paragraph!

Just kidding...yes, there will be interviews that don't result in an offer. But if you apply my strategies and follow up properly with your interviewers and hiring managers, you'll not only come across as confident and knowledgeable, you'll create demand for yourself. You'll leave them convinced they need you on their team. Instead of desperately chasing them down for feedback, you'll be receiving the offer you've been working so hard to get!

CHAPTER 13

FULL COURT PRESS: NEGOTIATING YOUR OFFER

"In baseball and in business, there are three types of people. Those who make it happen, those who watch it happen, and those who wonder what happened."

~ TOMMY LASORDA, MLB HALL OF FAME PLAYER AND MANAGER

CONGRATULATIONS--YOU'VE JUST GOTTEN A CALL from your recruiter or the hiring manager: they're making you an offer!

Right after that, for many people...panic sets in. It shouldn't. Not if you've prepared for this conversation.

It can be challenging to negotiate your own compensation package, unless you go in ready for all possible hurdles and curveballs. This chapter will put you in the right frame of mind to handle the offer stage with confidence.

Remember that an offer is proof of a company's strong interest in you, not just for the next week, month or year, but ideally for many years; once you've been trained and have settled into your role, the cost of replacing you will be significant.

If they think you really want the job and will likely accept it on their initial terms, they may offer you a compensation package that will save them money. But they almost always have flexibility (on both money and benefits) because they're reluctant to move to their second or third choice of candidate, and because they want to avoid going through the search process again.

You may feel vulnerable, but believe it or not, you've got the upper hand. Without getting cocky or overconfident, remind yourself that you're the right person for the position--and you're the one they've chosen. If you approach the negotiation process as a collaborative effort with the hiring manager to create the best package possible for both sides, it can be fairly easy to agree on a higher amount overall. Everything's negotiable!

Before you do anything, get clear on this one point:

Whether you receive it verbally or in writing:

Never accept an offer right away!

I'll repeat that. Never accept an offer right away. Not ever. Even if it's well above your expectations.

At the end of the compensation discussion, always ask if you can have a day or two to consider the offer. Tell them you'll reach out to the hiring manager and/or Human Resources with any questions.

And do NOT skip the negotiating phase.

FIVE CRITICAL QUESTIONS TO ASK DURING SALARY NEGOTIATION

1. DO YOU HAVE ANY FLEXIBILITY IN THAT NUMBER?

Even if the offer is above what you expected, thank them and immediately ask, "Do you have any flexibility with that amount?"

Many people go into salary negotiation believing that base salary or bonuses are set in stone. Wrong. Most managers have some wiggle room to use as they see fit. That's why it's important for you to have a target amount in mind.

If they tell you they may have some flexibility, respond back with the following: "Based on the research I've done comparing peer-level employees at competing companies, I was targeting $110,000."

Emphasis on the word "target." That means you would like to get to $110,000, but you'll likely "settle" for $105,000, clearly above your $95,000 offer but probably still within their budgeted salary range. Make sure your "target" number is high enough that if the manager comes in lower, you'll still be pleased with the outcome.

If you accept the first number they offer, you could be walking away from many thousands of dollars. That difference in pay can and will accumulate over time. For example, if you accept a base salary of $95,000, instead of negotiating for $100,000, that $5,000 you walked away from could have become $7,000 the following year and $10,000 the year after that. Bonuses are often a percentage of salary, so when you fail to negotiate the best offer, your losses continue to compound. Year after year you leave more money on the table.

2. How should I look at the total amount of the offer, including bonuses and benefits?

If, for example, you're offered a $95,000 base salary, and you have a bonus potential of 20%, then your total compensation potential is $114,000. (Don't forget to factor in the cost of insurance, taxes, 401K plans, etc.) The tendency is to say, "My total compensation is X," and then divide by 12 to look at your monthly income.

The smart play here is to think about how much you really need to net on a weekly, monthly and annual basis. Your overall compensation package includes several elements. Think about how you can mix and match them to meet your financial goals. If, for example, you need to take home $6000 a month after taxes, you'll want to net $10,000 a month, which equals $120,000 annually. So how can you get to that $120,000? Can you live on $100,000 plus a $20,000 bonus? Are you better off earning

$105,000 plus a $15,000 bonus? How much do you feel comfortable living on month-to-month or week-to-week? Remember that bonuses are often paid at year end or even a month or two into the following calendar year, so don't factor them into your monthly needs analysis.

Keep in mind also that the cost of your health, dental and vision insurance will typically be subtracted from your paycheck. Companies vary in terms of the coverage they offer, so look at the financial burden they absorb versus costs they pass on to you.

Will your new firm contribute to your 401k? If so, how much? If they allow you to contribute up to a certain percentage of your pay, ask how much the company will match and at what point the match kicks in. Some companies will delay matching your contributions for several months, depending on the level and timing of your hire.

Are there any pre-tax benefits, such as transit checks, parking vouchers, company car or gas mileage reimbursement? These questions need to be asked as you work through your negotiation phase.

For positions with substantial commission-based compensation, it's critical to understand the hiring manager's expectations, how often those commissions are paid and if your salary will be a draw against commission.

3. WHAT IS MY BONUS BASED ON?

Bonuses can be based on your personal performance, the performance of your group or the results of the company as a whole. They can also be fixed at a set amount.

Bonus payments are the most ambiguous elements of a compensation package, as they're often based on a wide array of multipliers and computations: manager temperament, company performance, your own perceived effort and contribution to the group and company, and other factors shrouded in a mysterious fog. Find out if they can provide you with an estimated bonus range, including an outline of how it will be computed for your position.

4. How are raises determined and when are they offered?

The timing of your hire will likely affect whether you'll be eligible for a salary review by the end of your first calendar year, after your first 12 months, or within a different time frame. This is also something you can attempt to negotiate, and the best way to approach it is to ask, "If my performance exceeds your expectations, will you consider adjusting my salary accordingly before the date you just mentioned?" These are important questions; if your potential employer doesn't raise them, bring them up yourself.

5. How will I be evaluated? How has that been handled in the past?

Every company has a distinct set of metrics for evaluating an employee's contributions. Some use a grading system that determines bonus levels, and some have specific questions (based on your group and company area) that your manager will need to answer when it comes time to determine your salary and bonus going forward. If you can gain any insight into how these are computed, you can use that intel to guide you through your tenure at the firm.

What else is negotiable?

If you sense that your hiring manager is not being as flexible as you'd hoped with either salary or bonus numbers, ask what else you can negotiate. If you're offered three weeks paid vacation, don't blink--ask if you can request four. They may have a corporate policy in place, but some companies are more flexible, and may prefer to give you an extra week of paid vacation rather than a higher salary. If they offer a 3% match on your 401k contributions, ask if they'll bump it up to 5%. That extra 2% will be the equivalent of an additional 2% on your bonus! If they hesitate over some of these requests, ask if you can work from home on occasion, if that's something you'd like to do.

Several other elements of your offer may be negotiable, including the use of a company car, pretax childcare, commuting costs, reimbursement for tuition, membership in industry associations and clubs, or attending conferences. Conference costs may be included in your package, but perhaps they won't be ready to send you until you ask for that to be part of your compensation.

A word of caution. If you're offered an up-front signing bonus, special payment or something similar (however they phrase it), it may come at the expense of your annual salary. I recommend you ask them to incorporate that into your base salary. If they decline, they might consider putting a portion towards your base. Do whatever you can within reason to get that initial base salary as high as possible, and remind yourself that every dollar now means several times that amount just a few years down the road.

As you probably know, the winner is always the one who gives a number and stops talking. The loser says a number and immediately begins to waver, saying something like, "but I can be flexible." When making your request, state a number, for example $110,000, and then don't make another peep. They'll react one way or the other, but they'll do so based on $110,000, not their original $95,000.

As you can see, much of the offer can be negotiated. When you've thought these things through in advance, you'll know how each payment will play out in the long term, and you'll be prepared to target higher numbers, with reasons to back up them up. Your argument will come across as sound and reasonable, not tied to the emotion of the moment.

HOW TO RESIGN FROM YOUR CURRENT JOB

A few thoughts about resigning to accept your ideal job.

> **Power play:**
>
> If you need a benchmark for your target number, visit one or more of these sites (or others like them) for general information and advice.
>
> www.payscale.com
> www.salary.com
> www.glassdoor.com

Walking into your manager's office to give notice can be challenging, even emotional, especially if you've become friendly over the course of your tenure there. Even though I followed the advice I'm about to give you, when I left the company I'd been with for 19 years, resigning to the owner of the firm was incredibly difficult and I struggled to find the right words. Here's what I did, and what I recommend you do to get past that difficulty.

Before you go into your manager's office, type up a letter that states you're giving notice but also reflects on your time in the job and ends with an offer to help make the transition easier:

Hello Richard,

I am officially giving my two weeks' notice today after accepting a position at another company.

For the past x years, I have enjoyed working at [Name of Company]. The people here have been a great influence, and I trust I was able to contribute to the company's success. I appreciate all you have done for me over the years, including your advice, insight and mentoring when I needed it.

If there is anything I can do to make the transition over the next two weeks any easier, please don't hesitate to ask.

My decision is final as I have put a tremendous amount of thought and effort into making this move. Thank you once again for everything.
Sincerely,
Mark

You'll notice that I started with my official resignation, followed by positive statements about my time at the company. Even if you had a miserable experience, make sure to come up with at least one or two positive elements you can mention. If you only liked a few of your co-workers, say "many of the people here." Even if you think most of them were not great co-workers, do not mention that in the letter! Follow with your offer to help during the transition, and end with the statement that your decision is final. You don't want to leave the door open for a counteroffer. Those are fraught with danger! Strong words, I know, but studies have shown that most people who accept a counteroffer to stay at a company are gone within six months. You might get fired or laid off soon after a replacement is found. Or the manager will make working conditions more challenging because you demonstrated a willingness to abandon the team. Bottom line...once you make that decision to go for your new adventure, stick to it. You'll be thrilled you did.

Congratulations--it's time to start your great new job in a company you're excited to join!

Stay In The Game

"It ain't over till it's over."

~ Yogi Berra, MLB Hall of Famer

The race is over, but the training continues...

WHAT A JOURNEY! BY FOLLOWING the *WIN AGAIN* playbook and working through the steps of this process, you've either landed a job in a position you hadn't even dreamt of a few short weeks ago, or you're laps ahead of the field as you near an offer (maybe more than one).

You've discovered a lot about what makes you tick, you've identified the skills and abilities you have that companies greatly value, and you learned how to put all that into a ten-to-fifteen-second answer to the inevitable question: *"What do you do?"*

Based on this much deeper understanding of what you want to do next, and within which kind of company and environment, you've created a list of positions to target. You set up or completely revitalized your LinkedIn profile and sent out numerous invitations to connect, adding many influential professionals to your network: key influencers and decision-makers able to help you land your new position, and, just as important, potential mentors who can assist you as you move forward on your new career path.

You're now comfortable performing at a high level within the interview process, winning the interviewer to your side with your ability to establish a strong rapport and transform the conversation into a productive dialogue.

What you learned may well have added thousands of dollars to the offers you receive, including one you've accepted--not only increasing the value of the work you do now, but also the amount you'll earn throughout the remainder of your career.

Even better, you've enhanced your networking capabilities. By anticipating what hiring managers want, you'll have a significant head start during the first three months at your new job. Continue to use the same strategies you've developed as you settle into your new role and keep adding LinkedIn connections to your expanding network.

Never stop applying the work ethic and mindset that helped you thrive as an athlete--they will serve you well. Given the strong foundation of your years in sports, and the strategies you've learned in this book, I have all the confidence in the world that you'll be a great success going forward!

ACKNOWLEDGEMENTS

THIS BOOK WOULD NEVER HAVE been written if not for those of you I've had the pleasure and honor to work with and advise over the years. It's been immensely satisfying to help each one of you, and I've benefited from all the insight and experiences you've offered in return.

Thanks to:

Greg Johnson, whose kind words about my impact on his job search and encouragement to focus on helping retired athletes inspired the direction of this book.

Ilona Chessid and Scott Rees, the dynamic duo of editing and guidance through the process. They prodded, cajoled and led me down the path, and I can't imagine anyone better qualified.

Desiree Desaulniers, who helped me write in bite sizes much of the content in *WIN AGAIN*. She's as organized and focused as it gets--the rudder in the wandering ship I often seemed to be.

Rob Carter, who did a stellar job of converting onto paper my vision for the artwork and designs for this book. He's an immensely talented illustrator, graphic designer and creative guy. More important, I consider him a great friend and a fellow NY Rangers diehard.

Ali Daggett, whose branding expertise and boundless energy gave me much-needed direction for both *WIN AGAIN* and my business.

Iliana Rivera, assistant extraordinaire, able to tackle every task I threw her way with great skill, all with a smile and constant encouragement.

Thanks again to all of you who have supported me and encouraged me to press on with *WIN AGAIN*. I can't wait to help as many of you as possible achieve your highest level of success and happiness!

ABOUT MARK MOYER

MARK MOYER IS UNIQUELY QUALIFIED to understand and address the challenges of current and retired professional or amateur athletes who want to launch a second career in the business world. With 25 years of experience in both recruiting and career coaching, he brings a unique dual perspective to the job search: he can think like a hiring manager at the same time as he motivates and develops a strategy for the candidate.

He's worked with people at all stages of their careers, from recent grads to seasoned executives, in a wide range of businesses. In recent years, Mark has combined his specialized expertise with a lifetime love of sports to meet the needs of a powerful but underserved population: those who have excelled as athletes and now want to transition to the corporate arena.

Mark is a frequent speaker and panelist at universities and career seminars, a Forbes contributor, widely quoted in a variety of business and sports-related publications, and remains an active member of Colgate University's alumni community. In addition to being a serial advice provider and idea generator, Mark enjoys playing ice hockey, softball, golf, guitar and piano, and coaching Little League baseball.

He lives in Manhattan with his wonderful wife and three amazing children.

CONNECT WITH MARK

Learn more about Mark and his WIN AGAIN Playbook,
and access additional resources here:
www.markmoyer.com

LinkedIn:
www.linkedin.com/in/1markmoyer/

Join his LinkedIn Group:
Mark Moyer | Career and Business Coach

Facebook:
www.facebook.com/MarkMoyerCoach/

Twitter:
@MarkMoyerCoach

Made in the USA
Columbia, SC
06 January 2020

86341671R00093